KU-091-446

being with flowers

Ou Baholyodhin and Erez Yardeni

DUNCAN BAIRD PUBLISHERS

LONDON

being with flowers

Ou Baholyodhin and Erez Yardeni

First published in the United Kingdom and Ireland in 2001 by
Duncan Baird Publishers Ltd
Sixth Floor
Castle House
75–76 Wells Street
London W1T 3QH

Conceived, created and designed by Duncan Baird Publishers

Copyright © Duncan Baird Publishers, 2001
Text copyright pages 8–189 © Ou Baholyodhin and Erez Yardeni, 2001
Text copyright pages 190–206 © Stephen Roberts, 2001
Commissioned photographs copyright © Duncan Baird Publishers, 2001
For copyright of all other photographs, see page 208
which is to be regarded as an extension of this copyright

The Authors' moral rights have been asserted in accordance with the
Copyright, Designs and Patents Act of 1988.

All rights reserved. No part of this publication may be reproduced or
utilized in any form or by any means electronic or mechanical,
including photocopying, recording, or by any information storage
and retrieval system now known or hereafter invented, without
the prior written permission of the Publisher.

Consultant: Stephen Roberts
Designer: Manisha Patel
Picture Researchers: Julia Brown, Alice Gillespie and Amy Kent
Commissioned photography: David Hiscock
Commissioned photography stylists: Ou Baholyodhin, with Robert Hornsby
of IN WATER (see page 208)

British Library Cataloguing-in-Publication Data:
A CIP record for this book is available from the British Library

ISBN: 1-903296-32-3

10 9 8 7 6 5 4 3 2 1

Typeset in Eurostile 10/20pt
Colour reproduction by Colourscan, Singapore
Printed and bound in Singapore by Imago

Publisher's Note:
Every attempt has been made to identify all the flowers in this book by
genus, species and variety. However, sometimes this has not been possible.
In these cases as much information as possible has been given.

to each other

contents

BEING WITH FLOWERS
INTRODUCTION BY OU BAHOLYODHIN

FLOWERS HAVE ALWAYS BEEN AN INTEGRAL PART OF MY WORK AS A DESIGNER AND TO DATE I HAVE NEVER COMPLETED A DESIGN PROJECT WITHOUT THE INCLUSION OF FLOWERS AT SOME POINT. MY NATURAL INSTINCT IS TO SURROUND MYSELF WITH FLOWERS. WITHOUT THEM I WOULD NOT FEEL "FULLY DRESSED", SO TO SPEAK. IN EVERY DESIGN PROJECT, WHETHER FOR AN INTERIOR, EVENT OR EXHIBITION, THE DAY I LOOK FORWARD TO THE MOST IS THE DAY OF COMPLETION. OF COURSE, TO SEE A PROJECT COMPLETED IS VERY SATISFYING, BUT THE FLOWERS ARE THE PART IN WHICH I TAKE THE GREATEST JOY. CERTAIN PROJECTS INSPIRE ME TO CREATE A DEDICATED FEATURE FOR FLOWERS – A SMALL INTERIOR GARDEN OR AN ALCOVE, PERHAPS, WHILE IN OTHER PROJECTS I DECIDE TO LEAVE THE FLOWERS TO THE LAST MINUTE FOR A MORE INSTINCTIVE AND SPONTANEOUS ARRANGEMENT.

THIS BOOK CELEBRATES THE JOY OF BEING WITH FLOWERS. FOR MANY PEOPLE FLOWERS HAVE A SPIRITUAL SIGNIFICANCE – HAVE YOU EVER NOTICED HOW NATURALLY AND SPONTANEOUSLY YOU RESPOND TO EVEN A SINGLE FLOWER IN A VASE; OR AN INVITING FIELD FULL OF BUTTERCUPS AND DAISIES IN SUMMERTIME? THIS NATURAL LINK IS WHAT MOVES US TO USE FLOWERS TO EXPRESS OUR THOUGHTS AND EMOTIONS. THROUGHOUT THE WORLD FLOWERS ARE PRESENTED AS OFFERINGS TO DEITIES; THEY FORM A VITAL PART OF THE RITUALS, CELEBRATIONS AND FESTIVITIES

OF MANY DIFFERENT CULTURES. THE ARRANGEMENTS VARY FROM INTRICATE STRINGS OF GARLANDS TO JUST A FEW SIMPLE PETALS FLOATING IN WATER. IN EASTERN RELIGIONS, FLOWERS REPRESENT THE UNFOLDING OF SPIRITUAL LIFE, SYMBOLIZED SPECIFICALLY BY THE LOTUS FLOWER. IN THIS BOOK WE CAPTURE THE SAME SPIRIT OF CELEBRATION AS WE OFFER A GLOBAL PERSPECTIVE ON THE PURE PLEASURE OF USING FLOWERS IN OUR HOMES.

THE VERY PRESENCE OF FLOWERS ANYWHERE IS ENOUGH TO MAKE MY FACE IMMEDIATELY LIGHT UP WITH JOY. WHAT COULD BE MORE DELIGHTFUL THAN COMING HOME TO A ROOM FILLED WITH THE HEADY SCENT OF JASMINE, OR GOING OUT INTO THE GARDEN AND BREATHING IN THE FRAGRANCE OF FRESH GARDENIAS AFTER RAINFALL? FEW OTHER SMALL GESTURES CAN COMPARE WITH THE SIMPLE ACT OF OFFERING FLOWERS, WHETHER THEY ARE A GIFT FOR YOURSELF, YOUR GUESTS OR YOUR HOME. IN INTERIORS FLOWERS ARE OFTEN ONE OF THE FIRST FEATURES TO BE NOTICED – I THINK BECAUSE THEY ARE OFTEN THE ONLY NATURAL FEATURE OF A ROOM – AND WE ARE INSTINCTIVELY DRAWN TO THEM. THEY MAKE YOUR HOME WARM, WELCOMING, VIBRANT AND ENERGIZED. AT THE SAME TIME, HOWEVER, FLOWERS CAN BE USED TO HELP CREATE CALM AND MEDITATIVE SPACES FOR RELAXATION AND CONTEMPLATION.

THE SIZE AND COMPLEXITY OF A FLOWER DISPLAY ARE NOT NECESSARILY WHAT MAKE IT SUCCESSFUL. WHAT COUNTS IS HOW YOU APPROACH YOUR DESIGN. A SINGLE BLOSSOM OF WHITE ROSE FLOATING IN A SIMPLE GLASS BOWL SPEAKS A THOUSAND WORDS. PRECIOUS, YET UNASSUMING, ITS SIMPLICITY AND PURITY EVOKE TRUTH AND WISDOM; IT IS PROUD YET GENTLE AND WELCOMING. WITH CARE AND SENSITIVITY MODEST ARRANGEMENTS CAN HAVE PROFOUND CONSEQUENCES ON OURSELVES AND OUR INTERIORS.

THIS IS NOT A STEP-BY-STEP GUIDE ON HOW TO ARRANGE FLOWERS, NOR IS IT A RECIPE BOOK THAT ATTEMPTS TO IMPART KNOWLEDGE THROUGH INSTRUCTIONS AND TIPS. *BEING WITH FLOWERS* IS NOT SPECIFICALLY ABOUT DISPLAYING FLOWERS IN EACH ROOM IN THE HOME – THERE IS NO GIVEN FORMULA FOR FLORAL DISPLAY IN THE BATHROOM, BEDROOM, KITCHEN AND SO ON.

BEING WITH FLOWERS IS ABOUT OUR INNER PERCEPTION OF FLOWERS AND HOW THEIR BEAUTY CAN ENHANCE OUR LIVES, OUR HOMES AND OUR SURROUNDINGS. I HOPE THIS BOOK ENCOURAGES YOU TO PAUSE SILENTLY FROM TIME TO TIME TO BECOME AWARE OF YOUR TRUE INNER NATURE, AND TO ENJOY THE SPONTANEITY AND INSIGHT OF EVERYDAY BEING.

DESIGN FOR THE SPIRIT

NATURALLY, I COULD NOT WRITE A BOOK ON CONTEMPORARY FLOWER ARRANGE-MENT IN INTERIORS WITHOUT ACKNOWLEDGING THE GREAT CULTURAL TRADITIONS. THESE TRADITIONS – AMONG THEM, EASTERN PRACTICES SUCH AS FENG SHUI AND ZEN, AND THE MOVEMENTS IN THE WEST SUCH AS MODERNISM – HAVE USED FLOW-ERS FOR A VARIETY OF PURPOSES FOR THOUSANDS OF YEARS. BUT THE MAGNIFICENT WELLSPRING WHICH IS THE HISTORICAL TRADITION OF FLOWERS IS NOT WHAT THIS BOOK IS ABOUT. INSTEAD, I HAVE TRIED TO DESCRIBE A MORE DIRECT EXPERIENCE OF USING FLOWERS: TO OFFER YOU AN INSIGHT INTO THE ASSOCIATIONS, FEELINGS, THOUGHTS AND SENSATIONS THAT EACH ARRANGEMENT OF FLOWERS, IN THEIR OWN PARTICULAR SETTING, HAS EVOKED IN ME.

WHAT DRIVES ME TOWARD A PARTICULAR SELECTION OF FLOWERS, VESSEL AND SET-TING IS COMMON TO US ALL: IT IS AN INSTINCTIVE RESPONSE TO AN INTERIOR, WHICH COMES FROM DEEP WITHIN AND WHICH FEELS SPONTANEOUSLY "RIGHT". FLOWERS ARE A VITAL PART OF OUR HOMES, AND OUR CHOICE OF FLOWERS AND THE WAY WE ARRANGE THEM IN OUR INTERIORS IS A MANIFESTATION OF OUR OWN INNER CREATIVITY. WE ALL HAVE THIS CREATIVITY – WE ARE BORN WITH IT; IT IS AN INTEGRAL PART OF US.

HOWEVER, AS EVERYDAY LIFE IN THE WEST CONTINUES TO GATHER PACE, WE OFTEN FEEL SO STRESSED OR SO PRESSURIZED THAT WE BECOME DISCONNECTED FROM THIS INNER CREATIVITY. AS A RESULT, PERHAPS, THE WEST IS LOOKING TO THE EAST FOR ANSWERS, FOR A WAY TO ESTABLISH A RECONNECTION. THIS PROCESS OF INTEGRATION AND CULTURAL INVESTIGATION PERMEATES THIS BOOK. INTERIORS DO NOT HAVE TO BE STEEPED IN TRADITIONAL EASTERN PHILOSOPHY OR EVEN BE VAGUELY ORIENTAL TO BE SYMBIOTIC – THEY JUST NEED THE RIGHT "SPIRIT". AT THE CORE OF THE BUDDHIST TRADITION, WHICH UNDERLIES ALL EASTERN THOUGHT, IS THE BELIEF THAT HAPPINESS COMES BY RECOGNIZING THE FUTILITY OF HUMAN NEED. IN OTHER WORDS, A CONSTANT STRIVING TO FULFIL OUR WANTS AND DESIRES WILL NOT BRING US CONTENTMENT. TRUE HAPPINESS LIES IN SIMPLY "BEING" – BEING TRUE TO OUR INNER NATURE. IN BUDDHISM THE ELIMINATION OF SUFFERING (AND ULTIMATELY REACHING A STATE OF BLISS) IS ACHIEVED THROUGH THE CONSTANT CULTIVATION OF CLEAR, PEACEFUL AWARENESS.

TO UNDERSTAND THIS FULLY WE NEED TO BE AWARE OF ONE FURTHER, CRUCIAL POINT ABOUT THE BUDDHIST DISTINCTION BETWEEN BEING AND THE SELF. BEING IS THE REALITY OF BOUNDLESS AWARENESS, OF CONSTANT CHANGE WITHOUT AN OBJECT OF CHANGE. CONVERSELY, THE SELF IS THE PERCEPTION OF REALITY FROM A

LIMITED POINT OF VIEW. WITHIN THIS LIMITATION, REALITY IS PERCEIVED AS SOME-THING MADE UP OF SELF AND OTHERS – OUR "SELF" IS SEPARATED FROM THE WORLD AND ALL OTHER EXISTENCE. IN BUDDHISM THERE IS SIMPLY BEING; THE SELF DOES NOT EXIST, BECAUSE IT IS A FULLY INTEGRATED, INSEPARABLE PART OF THE CONTI-NUITY OF LIFE. IN ESSENCE, THE BUDDHIST SPIRITUAL PATH IS THE PATH IN WHICH SUFFERING IS ELIMINATED BY DISPELLING THE DELUSION OF THE SELF AND BECOM-ING AWARE OF THE TRUE REALITY OF EXISTENCE.

FOR ME, DESIGNING WITH FLOWERS COMES FROM A STATE OF CONTINUED MEDITA-TION, A DEEP, MINDFUL AWARENESS OF A UNIFIED REALITY IN WHICH THERE IS NO NEED AND NO SUFFERING. EACH TIME YOU CHOOSE, ARRANGE AND DISPLAY FLOWERS, TRY TO SENSE A MOMENT OF PERFECTION WHEN YOU FEEL WHOLLY CONNECTED TO NATURE AND THE UNIVERSE – THIS IS A MOMENT OF PURE BEING.

OU BAHOLYODHIN

welcome

making a gesture for the visitor

WELCOME: MAKING A GESTURE FOR THE VISITOR

FLOWERS HAVE COME TO SYMBOLIZE ALMOST EVERY CONCEIVABLE IDEA IN BOTH THE EAST AND THE WEST, BUT ONE OF THE WAYS IN WHICH THEY MOST FREQUENTLY CONTRIBUTE TO OUR LIVES IS AS THE PERFECT, MOST EXPANSIVE, GESTURE OF WELCOME. WHEN WE FILL OUR HOMES WITH FLOWERS WE ARE PRESENTING A GIFT TO BOTH OUR VISITORS AND OURSELVES.

THE DESIGNS IN THIS CHAPTER HAVE NOT BEEN CONCEIVED AS MEANS TO IMPRESS OTHERS; NOR ARE THEY INTENDED TO ENCOURAGE YOU TO BE SELF-INDULGENT. RATHER, THEIR PURPOSE IS TO HELP YOU CREATE A CERTAIN ATMOSPHERE IN YOUR HOME. FOR EXAMPLE, IF YOU FOCUS MINDFULLY ON THE ACT OF ARRANGING THEM, YOUR RESPECTFUL ATTITUDE WILL SHINE THROUGH IN YOUR DISPLAYS. OR IF YOU DESIGN WITH PURITY AND TRANQUILLITY IN YOUR HEART, THESE QUALITIES WILL RESOUND THROUGHOUT YOUR LIVING SPACE AND BRING YOU PEACE.

IN A SERENE, WELCOMING, HOME ENVIRONMENT OUR SPIRITS ARE NATURALLY LIFTED AND OUR MINDS FREED FROM THE OPRESSIVE RULE OF NEGATIVE THOUGHTS. JUST AS INCENSE PURIFIES THE AIR IN TEMPLES, SO THE PERFUME OF FLOWERS CAN SANCTIFY OUR HOMES. THE SCENT OF JASMINE, TUBEROSES, LILIES AND OTHER FRAGRANT BLOSSOMS ARE PERFECT CHOICES.

SINCE TIME IMMEMORIAL FLOWERS HAVE BEEN USED IN RELIGIOUS CELEBRATIONS AND RITUALS, PRIZED PARTICULARLY FOR THEIR PURIFYING SCENT AND BEAUTIFUL BLOSSOMS. TODAY, THROUGHOUT THE WORLD, FLOWERS STILL PLAY AN INTEGRAL ROLE IN THE FESTIVITIES AND CELEBRATIONS OF MANY DIFFERENT CULTURES, OFTEN HAVING SPECIAL, SPIRITUAL SIGNIFICANCE. FOR EXAMPLE, BRAHMA AND THE BUDDHA ARE FREQUENTLY DEPICTED EMERGING FROM LOTUS FLOWERS; THE DOVE-LIKE COLUMBINE REPRESENTS THE HOLY SPIRIT; AND THE VIRGIN MARY IS OFTEN SHOWN HOLDING A LILY OR AN IRIS. THE CHINESE NEW YEAR IS WHEN THE DELICATE NARCISSUS BLOOMS – A FLOWER THAT, ACCORDING TO ORIENTAL TRADITION, SIGNIFIES JOY, GOOD LUCK OR A HAPPY MARRIAGE.

FLOWERS MAKE ALL KINDS OF CELEBRATIONS SPECIAL AND CREATE AN IMPRESSIVE BACKDROP TO OUR MOST SIGNIFICANT RITES OF PASSAGE, SUCH AS WEDDINGS, ANNIVERSARIES AND CHRISTENINGS. BUT EVEN AN EVERYDAY MEAL IS TRANS-FORMED INTO A CELEBRATION IF IT IS SERVED AT A TABLE ADORNED WITH A FEW BLOSSOMS, SUCH AS LILIES, JASMINE, ROSES AND GERBERAS, WHICH ARE SOME OF THE MOST POPULAR FLOWERS IN CONTEMPORARY ARRANGEMENT. WHATEVER THE OCCASION, FLOWERS BRING JOY INTO OUR LIVES, PERSISTING FRAGRANTLY IN OUR MEMORIES LONG AFTER THE BLOOMS THEMSELVES HAVE FADED AWAY.

RIGHT: *Dianthus caryophyllus* hybrids 'Scania'   OPPOSITE: *Dianthus caryophyllus* hybrids 'Sorento'

contemporary garland

Different arrangements emphasize different qualities of flowers, their vibrant colours, their leaf and petal shapes, and so on. Some of the most stunning effects are created when we emphasize the most powerful feature of the flowers. One of the most successful ways of doing this is to mass pure blooms (or leaves) of the same plant together. In Asia, hundreds of jasmines are assembled into intricate garland strings, worthy as offerings to deities. Similarly, stems of the aromatic bay species of laurel were gathered together and used in magnificent crowns for ancient Greek warriors and poets. In both these cases the flowers and/or leaves cease to be individual stems: they form a beautiful, striking whole.

The confident treatment of these vibrant carnation balls extracts and plays up their most pleasing elements – pure colour and the exquisite depth of their velvety texture. Displayed in a polished plaster panel, the petals of each flower head dissolve into one another, losing their individual character entirely. The result – three striking spheres – has far more impact than simply a loose collection of stems gathered together in a vase.

BELOW AND OPPOSITE: *Forsythia* x *intermedia*

drama and symmetry

Imagine the immediate thrill and joy of a visitor to your home as they enter the hallway and catch their first glance of these amazing arrangements. Sweeping branches of bright gold forsythia, the essence of spring, capture that first moment of excitement on entering a friend's home – and these arrangements are unlikely to be overlooked or forgotten. Their expansive curves echo the arched doorways. The dramatic stems are complemented by their placement in a pair of magnificent sculptural vases.

For theatrical effect, accentuated by vibrant colour and form, put together a gigantic arrangement of large exuberant flowers. Let yourself go as you build your design but remember to keep its colour and shape balanced and harmonious. Yellow – on walls, in the painting and in the flowers' blooms – is the unifying theme here. Flamboyant containers avoid any pompous formality in the interior and add the finishing touch.

"Whoever holds in their mind the great image of oneness, the world will come to them. It will flow and not be obstructed – coming in safety, oneness and peace."

Tao Te Ching

open archways

This modest and minimal interior reflects the vogue for pared-down living. The purity and clarity of the room encourage the same qualities to develop in your mind-stream. In this modern apartment the open design of the stairway allows sunlight to flood in, adding warmth to the metal and concrete features.

Bay trees in terracotta pots were traditionally placed on either side of a doorway to greet guests entering a home. Here, however, this tradition has been updated with a pair of majestic cacti set in concrete, gravel-filled containers. The cacti are more in line with the stark architecture, and with modern interior design in general. Although they may seem harsh plants to offer in welcome, the cacti display an asymmetry (the tall versus the short), which is somehow softening, and the warm light from the window is comforting to the entering visitor.

OPPOSITE: *Echinocactus grusonii* ABOVE: *Euphorbia eritraea*

arranging with light

Light affects us just as much as colour and space in the home, and can be used to display and enhance the full beauty of flowers. Natural light is the welcoming focus and soul of any room, and similar to the way in which back-lighting is used in the painting of an old master, back-lighting (below) reveals the translucency of spray rose petals and frames an arrangement at a window. In contrast, light is used to express the solidity of the arrangement (opposite).

Painters use light in their work to enhance the sense of volume. By positioning flowers to make the most of the available light, you can play up the solidity of an arrangement or reveal its translucency. In this way, light becomes a part of the arrangement. Decide in advance how you want to display your flowers: side- or back-lighting achieves volume and the most dramatic effects.

OPPOSITE: *Rosa 'Escapade'* ABOVE: *Asclepias, Euphorbia, Matthiola*

THIS PAGE: *Dahlia* OPPOSITE: *Paeonia*

ABOVE: *Alpinia zerumbet, Heliconia pendula* 'Sexy Pink', *Monstera deliciosa* OPPOSITE: *Anthurium andraeanum* 'Choco' and 'Midori'

altar celebration

An overwhelming display of colourful tropical flowers – heleconia, ginger, palm and monstera leaves – suggests a festive occasion (opposite). The addition of a symbol of renewed life, purity and goodness, such as the Buddha statue, enhances the celebratory feeling and at the same time sets the mood of our home as a place of kindness, tranquillity and perfection. When we see a garland placed directly in front of a Buddha image, we feel it is an act of offering: one of ritual and of respect. However, when the arrangement is placed to one side of the Buddha, it no longer becomes an offering to the image but to the interior and to ourselves.

A quieter, more restrained and contemplative mood is reflected in the arrangement of anthuriums (above). Shrine-like, the design fulfils the basic human need to retreat to a quiet corner to meditate. As life becomes more hectic, age-old rituals become more meaningful and flowers can help to transform your home into a sanctuary from the outside world.

RIGHT: *Ligustrum japonicum, Rudbeckia nitida* OPPOSITE: *Laurus nobilis, Rudbeckia nitida*

"Something is mysteriously brought into existence

... It is silent and shapeless,

It is always present, endlessly in motion."

Lao Tzu

alchemy

The same flowers are used in both of these rooms for surprisingly different effects: below, the flowers and trees are presented in a hallway in a symmetrical fashion – almost like a formal Italian garden. Opposite, the arrangement seems more relaxed and informal. However, both displays are juxtaposed with features of the interior that strike a paradoxical note. In the hallway below, the formal display is set upon an informal, collapsible table. Furthermore, the flowers themselves are placed in an old metal water jug. In the display shown opposite, the informal flower arrangement is offset not only by the topiary trees behind it, but also by the chandelier which hangs from the ceiling. Here, the overall effect is more imposing than we might first imagine.

LEFT: *Viburnum opulus* 'Sterile' OPPOSITE: *Viburnum opulus* 'Sterile',
Zantedeschia 'Green Goddess'

freshness

Green is a soothing shade and ideal for use in entrances and hallways, where it brings an air of freshness that is both spiritually uplifting and purifying. Restful and reassuring, the colour green will encourage your guests to relax and enjoy themselves in your home.

In both of these photographs, round blooms of green guelder rose are casually arranged in a slender glass container. Their dark green leaves provide the ideal tonal contrast of green on green. The vase is almost invisible; attention is concentrated on flowers and stems alone. The guelder rose is a wonderful shrub and the cut blooms look beautiful in almost any combination of flowers and foliage. In the fall, the flower heads are a mass of rich, vibrant red.

essence of flowers

White is a symbol of purity, truth and the sacred or divine. Similarly, the white rose is an emblem of innocence and virtue. Single white roses floating in glass bowls or presented on a shallow plate have a purifying effect on ourselves and our interiors. Pared down to their simplest form, the flower heads are without leaves or stems, leaving us with just the essence of flowers.

Beyond the flowers is no other decoration. To add more leaves would blemish their clarity. These arrangements are personal and inward-looking: they are not meant to change the appearance of a room but to create a subtle, clean and calm moment in your day. The roses are not displayed in vases. Presented in this way they are more of an offering to yourself and your guests. Unassuming, yet careful, they are quiet and peaceful; cleansing and purifying.

OPPOSITE AND ABOVE: *Rosa* 'Bianca'

a pure intention

The act of making an offering to your guests is a genuine gesture and it is appropriate that such flower arrangements should be kept plain and unassuming. Large and complex flower arrangements would be too flamboyant and impersonal here.

If the intention is pure and good, and the arrangement really comes from the giver's heart, then it is sufficient to place a single blossom on a simple plate. This humble and sincere gesture speaks more than a thousand words.

ABOVE: *Paeonia* OPPOSITE (ABOVE): *Rosa* cultivars OPPOSITE (BELOW): *Camellia japonica*

THIS PAGE: *Allium, Dahlia* OPPOSITE: *Dahlia, Ranunculus*

drawing in the light

Artificial light can appear cool and lifeless in an interior. When flowers are introduced, however, the qualities of light – natural or artificial – are enhanced. In both these interiors, yellow stems of foxtail lily seem almost like strong shafts of sunlight which cast their warm glow over the orderly arrangement of interesting artifacts.

Choose flowers to complement the existing lighting in your home. Warm, bright colours add liveliness and brilliance to your rooms. Simply position your arrangement in the same way you would a table lamp or any other light source. Remember, the more flowers you use, or the larger the arrangement you decide to create, the brighter the effect will be.

"By your grace I remember my Light,

and now my delusion is gone."

Bhagavad Gita

ALL PHOTOGRAPHS: *Eremurus*

movement

creating fluidity in space

MOVEMENT: CREATING FLUIDITY IN SPACE

YOUR HOME IS A LIVING, BREATHING ENTITY WITH A SOUL. TO ASSIST THE FLOW OF ENERGY AND MOVEMENT IN YOUR HOME (JUST AS IN YOUR OWN SELF), IT IS IMPORTANT TO LOOK AFTER THE WELL-BEING OF THAT SOUL. OUR MINDS, BODIES AND SPIRITS NEED TO BE CARED FOR AND CONSTANTLY NURTURED TO MAINTAIN GOOD HEALTH. SIMILARLY, OUR HOMES WILL BENEFIT FROM: A REGULAR ROUTINE OF CLEANSING AND TIDYING FOR GOOD PHYSICAL ORDER; DE-CLUTTERING AND REARRANGING TO MAINTAIN A CLEAR AND BALANCED INTERIOR COMPOSITION; AND, TO KEEP THE SPIRIT OF THE HOME ALIVE AND WHOLE, A CONTINUOUS FLOW OF ENERGY OR MOVEMENT.

FRESH FLOWERS AND PLANTS INTRODUCE DIFFERENT LEVELS OF MOVEMENT INTO YOUR HOME. EVERY CURVING STEM, EVERY LEAF AND EVERY PETAL OF A FLOWER REPRESENTS GROWTH AND THE INHERENT MOVEMENT OF THE NATURAL WORLD. A FLOWER IS JUST A SMALL PART OF THE TREE OR PLANT FROM WHICH IT GREW, YET ITS GREATER SIGNIFICANCE IS TO MOVE THE SPIRIT OF THE OUTSIDE INSIDE. FLOWERS TRANSPORT US FROM OUR IMMEDIATE SURROUNDINGS TO DIFFERENT PLACES WHERE THEY HAVE ASSOCIATIONS. FOR EXAMPLE, AN ARRANGEMENT OF TROPICAL FLOWERS AND LEAVES TRANSFORMS AN INTERIOR INTO AN EXOTIC SPACE, FAR FROM EVERY-THING THAT IS USUAL OR MUNDANE.

WHILE SOME DESIGN ELEMENTS, SUCH AS MAN-MADE FURNITURE, CAN HAVE A STATIC PRESENCE IN AN INTERIOR, FLOWERS ARE THE LIVING COMPONENTS OF ANY DESIGN, AND (THROUGH THEIR WEALTH OF COLOURS AND DIFFERENT SHAPES AND FORMS) THEY IMMEDIATELY BRING TO OUR ATTENTION THE FLOW OF ENERGY AND VITALITY IN A ROOM. THE EFFECT OF MOVEMENT IS THE SAME, WHETHER ARRANGEMENTS ARE PART OF AN OVERALL THEME OR DECORATIVE ELEMENTS IN THEMSELVES.

SPIRITUALLY, THE FLOWER IS A CONCISE SYMBOL OF NATURE AT ITS MOST PERFECT AND REPRESENTS THE CONSTANT CYCLE OF LIVING: BIRTH, LIFE, DEATH AND REBIRTH – A CONTINUOUS FLOW OF THE MOVEMENT OF LIFE; THE PROPER, NATURAL ORDER OF THINGS. THE BLOSSOMING AND EVENTUAL WILTING OF FLOWERS REMIND US OF OUR OWN EXISTENCE. AS NATURE KEEPS MOVING IN A FLOWER, SO IT DOES IN US. A GROWING FLOWER NEEDS CONSTANT NOURISHMENT AND RE-ENERGIZING THROUGH LOVE, CARE AND ATTENTION – OUR OWN NEEDS IN MICROCOSM. LET FLOWERS INTO YOUR HOME, LET THEIR BEAUTY AND FRAGRANCE BE A CONSTANT REMINDER THAT WITHIN US IS A DEEP NEED FOR MOVEMENT; LET THEM BE A SENSUOUS REPRESEN-TATION OF THE PARADOXICAL BELIEF THAT STILLNESS IS ACHIEVED THROUGH THE CONSTANT FLOW OF ENERGY, AND THAT CALM IS REACHED THROUGH VITALITY.

LEFT: *Xanthorrhoea australis* OPPOSITE: *Alocasia* and *Xanthorrhoea australis*

signposts in leaves

Flower arrangements should not be treated merely as ornaments; they are one of our closest everyday links with nature. A flower, leaf or stem breathes life into a space and creates a positive visual presence. In an urban home a single elephant leaf is a powerful statement – a bold reminder of nature in a tropical setting – and the steel grass reminds us of an open marshland. The shape of an arrangement can be directional: a signpost pointing toward another realm – beyond the window or into another room – reassuring us of the continuity of space from the inside to the outside of the home. The linear silhouette of fine blades of steel grass punctuates the internal space in a fountain of movement, which takes our eyes in a dome toward the skies and all the cardinal directions. We become aware of the infiniteness of space. Then, as the arrangement points us away from itself again, we experience a movement in our minds – a pure flow, which is our awareness and consciousness.

colour and vitality

Energizing and confident, red automatically brings vitality into our interiors. The invigorating properties of certain flowers can have similar effects. On these pages fluid arching stems of lilies are manifestations of playfulness and youth. Within each of the glass vases, every stem swings and sways freely. The flowers refuse to conform to human regularization.

To fully appreciate the movement in flowers, accept and enjoy them just as they are, for their natural charm and their stimulating qualities. Chinese lanterns (above) hang wilfully and haphazardly from long linear stems. These pods will not be trained into organized rows. Choose the flowers you identify with instinctively and give in to your instinct; let it lead you.

OPPOSITE AND ABOVE (RIGHT): *Zantedeschia* species and cultivars ABOVE (LEFT): *Physalis alkekengi* 'Franchetii'

creating space

Even a large room can feel oppressive and claustrophobic if it has little natural light, few windows and a low ceiling, whereas a smaller light-filled interior with high ceilings appears open and airy. Through their structure and colour some flowers convey a sense of space. When looking at such flowers you are filled with an inner sense of openness. This sense is transferred into the interior. So, by introducing flowers that convey space through their appearance, the room itself becomes spacious.

"The almighty sky does not hinder white clouds in their flight."

Ryokan

ABOVE: *Arundinaria* OPPOSITE: *Anethum graveolens*

dynamic composition

In our lives there are inevitably quiet moments when we want to retreat, and times of joy, which we want to share, and fill with the laughter of others. These moments are part of the natural dynamic flow of our spiritual energy. In our homes the same movement can be recreated through colours, textures, shapes and forms. Complex processes performed by the brain allow us to perceive a room immediately by scanning through the space and noting individual objects. The eye is led around the space, from one prominent object to the next. Here, two-dimensional images framed in a photograph allow greater understanding of the dynamics of an interior.

The circle is the recurring form (above) and features most prominently in the white glass lampshade in the centre of the room. From there, our gaze is drawn forward to the low table lamp, another object with a similar shape. Our eyes then travel across the room to the circular vase of lilies and finally rest on the painting of circular forms. On a smaller scale (opposite), fuchsia-pink and red books, a vase filled with colourful ranunculus and an abstract painting form a dynamic, almost classical, still-life composition. As our eyes move about the room, from one focal point to the next, so the energy of the room resonates within us.

OPPOSITE: *Lilium 'Casa Blanca', Palmacae family* RIGHT: *Eucalyptus globulus, Ranunculus*

"How can I be still? By flowing with the stream."

Lao Tzu

the artist's palette

When bold colour is introduced into the fabric of any interior it creates a powerful backdrop for the display of flowers. Nevertheless, it is not just large arrangements, or unusual flowers, that can hold their own in such a bright environment. Arresting effects can be achieved through clever choice, arrangement and placement of any kind of flower. Positioned with consideration, a single flower can be highly significant. For example, the white lily (opposite) in a tall sinuous vase immediately creates a sense of movement within the red and green hallway. Strong contrast in colour and form accentuates the effect.

Brightly coloured rooms can give interiors freshness and liveliness. The effect may be enhanced or balanced by using flowers. Green, for example, is said to have a calming effect. Throughout time artists have applied these principles of using colour to enhance mood in their paintings to great effect. Paul Cézanne (1839–1906) used a combination of pink and green in many of his paintings.

Generally you can use contrasting colours to create arrangements to suit your home but remember that it is the subtle differences in shades and textures of various flowers that conveys the feeling of a finely-tuned interior.

OPPOSITE (ABOVE): *Gerbera jamesonii* hybrids, *Lilium* cultivars, *Solidago* OPPOSITE (BELOW): *Dahlia* mixed cultivars LEFT: *Zantedeschia* species and cultivars

OPPOSITE: *Dahlia* LEFT: *Delphinium cultivar*

"Let everything be allowed to do what
it naturally does, so that its nature
will be satisfied."

Chuang Tzu

broken colours

The Impressionist movement (1860s–1880s) was a light, spontaneous manner of painting that began in France as a reaction to the formalism of the dominant Academic style. One of its principal innovations was a new way of using colour. The artist sought to depict seemingly uniform zones of colour through numerous strokes of different shades of paint juxtaposed against each other. An image could be seen only from a distance when the array of pure pigments was rearranged in the brain. The result was fresh and vibrant. Flowers too can be used as artist's oils or watercolours, the hue of each petal equivalent to the painter's dot of colour (left). In this way, single flowers disappear into the overall floral composition. Use flowers of a similar form and keep the arrangement as a solid whole; avoid focusing on individual flowers. Experiment with unexpected combinations; you may be surprised to discover how different shades work together to alter your perception of the component colours. Avoid hesitancy or this will come across in your work; be bold and enjoy the experience.

The curvaceous vase (opposite) is reminiscent of the work of the Catalan architect Antoni Gaudí (1852–1926). Gaudí developed a sensuously curving, almost surreal style with little regard for formality, and used colourful ceramic fragments to cover the interior and exterior of many of his buildings.

OPPOSITE: *Dianthus barbatus, Ornithogalum arabicum, Paeonia, Ranunculus*   LEFT: *Rosa 'Ambience'*

accentuating details

One simple way to create a more fluid mood in an interior is to add or replace a few accent pieces. For example, red silk pillows scattered around a white room immediately create a lively exotic atmosphere. Using texture as well as colour heightens the effect, and this can be echoed in your choice of flowers. Curving tulip stems add sensuality to an interior (below). A similarly sumptuous statement is achieved through a low arrangement of lustrously flared lilies or a few dahlia heads, their intense velvety petals hinting at mystery and opulence.

63

OPPOSITE: *Tulipa* 'Flaming Parrot'   LEFT (ABOVE): *Zantedeschia* species and cultivars   LEFT (BELOW): *Dahlia* species and cultivars

hallucination

Some interiors are almost unreal. Surfaces and colours that would not usually work together become a perfect whole. These idiosyncratic interiors are held together through personal vision. They are private dream worlds which are perfectly coherent in themselves but not in relation to design conventions. For example, aged brick walls (above) are the perfect backdrop to a rough-hewn oak table. Stainless-steel surfaces are complemented by abstract arrangements of papyrus, their sharp green projecting a glossy radiance and brash youthful energy. The vases blend almost seamlessly with the metal, and attention focuses on the grass.

ALL PHOTOGRAPHS: *Cyperus papyrus*

stepping stones

Careful positioning of identical plants or flowers within an interior affects how we perceive the space and shifts attention across the room. A grass trough (opposite, above) directs us to the far wall, where matching arrangements of the same grass are grouped together in a different fashion. The effect is like a visual stepping stone. Our eyes are drawn naturally from like to like. Containers and accessories can be used to enhance the effect, although these pointers do not need to be repeated in the same element or material. Visual interaction between the black monolithic vases in the background and the black table runner in the foreground is instinctive.

By taking a step back and treating an interior as a three-dimensional canvas we start to relate to its dynamism. The coconut palm (above) can be viewed simply as a solid object placed in the centre of the table but it also has a two-stage effect within the three-dimensional canvas. First, we see it as a lofty device, focusing our attention on the foreground, then it becomes transparent as our gaze drifts beyond.

OPPOSITE: *Cocos nucifera* BELOW: *Carex*

"Do not seek to follow in the
footsteps of the ancient ones;
seek what they sought."

Basho

modesty

designing with quiet attentiveness

MODESTY: DESIGNING WITH QUIET ATTENTIVENESS

IN INTERIOR DESIGN "MODESTY" MEANS DESIGNING WITH A LIGHTNESS OF TOUCH, WITH SIMPLICITY, CLARITY AND AWARENESS – IN OTHER WORDS, LISTENING AND RESPONDING TO AN INTERIOR. LIFE IS A CONSTANT EBB AND FLOW OF ACTIVITY AND A CONTINUOUS STRUGGLE TO EXPRESS AND FULFIL OURSELVES. SOMETIMES THIS CAN BE OVERWHELMING AND MAY PREVENT US FROM DISCOVERING TRUE FREEDOM: PEACE AND HAPPINESS WITHIN. AS RAPIDLY CHANGING THOUGHTS AND EMOTIONS RACE THROUGH OUR MINDS, MEDITATION HELPS US TO TAKE A DETACHED VIEW SO WE BECOME MORE IN TUNE WITH OURSELVES AND ACHIEVE GREATER BALANCE. LIKE A NATURAL STREAM, A SUBTLE CURRENT OF CONSTANT CHANGE FLOWS WITHIN US. THEREFORE, IT IS IMPORTANT TO CREATE SPACES IN THE HOME WHERE WE CAN RELAX. SURROUNDING OURSELVES WITH SIMPLE ARRANGEMENTS OF FRESH FLOWERS SUCH AS SNOWDROPS OR LILIES CAN ALSO BE UPLIFTING. THE BEAUTY OF THEIR COLOUR, TEXTURE AND SCENT AWAKENS AND REVITALIZES THE SENSES.

FLOWERS ARE AN ALMOST INDISPENSABLE ELEMENT OF A MEDITATIVE SPACE. THE JAPANESE ZEN GARDEN AND THE ZEN TEA CEREMONY ROOM ARE TWO OF THE BEST EXAMPLES OF THIS. EACH OF THESE SPACES INCLUDES A *TOKONOMA* WHICH IS, IN A SENSE, A SECULAR SHRINE. WITHIN THE *TOKONOMA* A SEASONAL BLOSSOM WILL ALMOST CERTAINLY BE FEATURED.

MEDITATIVE SPACES IN OUR HOMES ARE QUIET PLACES, EMPTIED OF CLUTTER, FORM, COLOUR AND TEXTURE. THEY GIVE THE IMPRESSION OF SIMPLICITY, YET THEY ARE NOT SIMPLIFIED. OUR HOMES NEED TO BE ARRANGED AS BALANCED ENVIRON-MENTS WHERE THE UNDERLYING SYMMETRY IS REVITALIZED, AND FLOWERS HAVE AN ESSENTIAL, DYNAMIC ROLE TO PLAY IN THIS PROCESS.

THE CHARACTERISTICS OF THE FLOWERS WITHIN THIS CHAPTER ARE THOSE OF SIMPLICITY, SUBTLE COLOURING, PERFECT BALANCE, HARMONY OF FORM. PERHAPS MORE THAN ANYTHING, THEY ARE FLOWERS WHICH EXUDE AN ABUNDANT, YET FRAGILE LIFE FORCE. TO ACHIEVE MODESTY, FLOWERS SHOULD BE ARRANGED SIMPLY AND WITH A FOCUSED AND QUIET MIND. THE RESULT IS AN ARRANGEMENT WHICH IS A LIVING ICON, SHIFTING OUR THOUGHTS AWAY FROM MATERIALISTIC AND WORLD-LY CONCERNS TO A MORE SERENE EXISTENCE.

"Wordiness and intellection;

the more we cling to them,

the further astray we go."

Hui-neng

quiet perfection

Minimalism is often described as being the state of perfection, the point at which no more can be added or subtracted without causing some degree of degradation. In this minimalist room the careful leaning of the alliums shows a complete respect toward the perfectly-conceived wishbone dining chairs. A sense of harmony is achieved through the entire "composition". The effect is so perfect that there is nothing that could be added or taken away.

This interior is calm and peaceful because there is no conflict of colour or form. It is pure and modest to the point where no element could be replaced. The pale translucent vase fades almost seamlessly into a background of white walls, while the gently curving allium stems echo the elegant lines of the furniture.

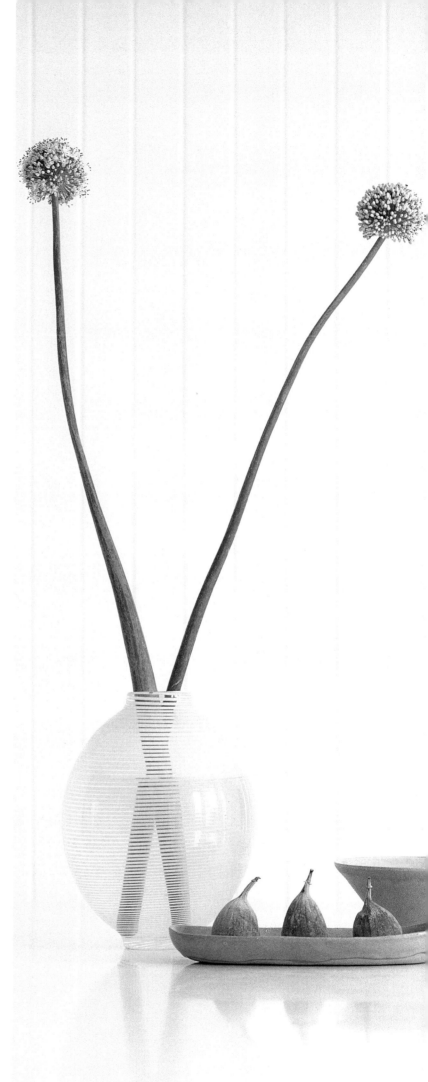

OPPOSITE AND RIGHT: *Allium*

ALL PHOTOGRAPHS: *Zantedeschia* 'Mango'

serenity and harmony

The arrangement shown on the opposite page (and in detail, above) represents a statement of balance and restraint. It owes its success to the careful way in which all the visual elements have been considered. While the vase is large and could be seen as extravagant, this would be to deny its more subtle aspects: its gentle curves and surfaces. Lilies add colour, yet the clear and delicate wavy lines of their elongated stems are poised and balanced. In a pared-down harmony of heaviness and lightness, the vase and flowers are a continuation of each other. Their complete interdependence introduces an underlying sense of quiet harmony.

"When all desires are in peace
... let the seeker quietly lead
the mind into the Spirit and
let all his thoughts be
silence."

Bhagavad Gita

THIS PAGE: *Ranunculus*

RIGHT: *Prunus, Rosa* 'Nicole' OPPOSITE: *Rosa* 'Nicole', *Tulipa* 'White Dream'

objets trouvés

There is a sense of the overtly feminine in this environment – it presents itself as an open display of traditional female insignia (pink fabrics, floral patterns, a lightness of touch). Understatement, diffusing the grandeur of the apartment, is achieved in the juxtaposition of simple and grand objects: a used soda can beside a wine carafe; simple fresh flowers (tulips, roses and spring blossoms) in front of an antique Venetian cut-glass mirror.

The designer's complex and subtle choice of arrangement results in a room that is simple in decoration, yet lofty in design. Unassuming flowers combined with opulent rococo furnishings translate into a comforting ideal. At this point a delicate balance between the intricate and simplistic elements, the ornate and the ordinary, is achieved to result in satisfying harmony.

ABOVE: *Viburnum fragrans* OPPOSITE: *Dahlia* species and cultivars

the music of flowers

A Zen master might say that the Japanese flute (*shakuhachi*) is capable of producing virtually every sound in existence, yet it is the notes we cannot hear that make it a Zen instrument. The Komuso, Japanese mendicant monks who walked in the wilderness, playing their *shakuhachi*, believed that one day they would create a single perfect sound: the sound of enlightenment. Interiors have their own natural harmony of sounds: textures join light and colour to resonate together.

Flowers are not silent. Like symphonies, some arrangements are bold and expansive, while others have the formality of chamber music. In this interior, delicate spring blossoms (opposite) float like suspended notes of music. Dahlia heads (above) float in perfect harmony in a simple stone bowl. Their tranquillity is the moment of silence in between notes. It is the stillness of the Buddha.

bamboo

If I had to choose a favourite plant, it would be the bamboo. The greenness of fresh bamboo is more intense than any other plant; its linear trunk straighter, its soft, matt surface more pure. Yet it is a simple grass, unassuming, quietly pleasing, and undemanding in interiors – as well as (on a practical level) being easy to maintain. For me, in every part of the bamboo lies perfection.

There is an old Japanese saying that the sound of clashing bamboo is the sound of enlightenment. If you have ever heard this sound, you will understand why the adage came about: it is a unique noise – clear and resonant; fresh and pure.

OPPOSITE: *Agave americana* (right), *Phyllostachys* (left) LEFT: *Phyllostachys*

LEFT AND RIGHT: *Eucharis grandiflora* 'Amazonica'

"Cloud above lotus—

it too

becomes a Buddha."

Boryu

the energy of space

Just as our minds and bodies enjoy the benefits of holistic techniques such as yoga, our homes too can be enhanced through the use of natural remedies. Think of your home as a living, breathing space with volume and soul. In meditation a sense of peacefulness inside is achieved when we become aware of a focus within ourselves. In a similar way, a focal point can be introduced within a home. Decide which is the pivotal room of the house. Imagine: you can funnel the energy from around your home into a central reservoir. In interior design it is crucial to maintain the focus of the home. In both of the interiors shown on these pages, long-stemmed flowers and foliage in tall vases achieve that aim, drawing in the surrounding space to meet in a single point – not at the flowers themselves, but where the stems cross within the vase.

"Without going outdoors one knows the world ...

The further out one goes, the lesser one's

knowledge becomes."

Tao Te Ching

OPPOSITE: *Agapanthus* 'Alba', *Cymbidium* cultivars, *Monstera deliciosa*, *Xanthorrhoea australis*, *Zantedeschia* species and cultivars
ABOVE: *Agapanthus* 'Blue Triumphator'

ALL PHOTOGRAPHS: *Allium*

single-point concentration

In this serene interior, flowers offer the only colour. The uniformity of tones, the pale wood, the white walls and furniture all speak of quiet restraint. Heads of allium arranged in a simple glass container present a focal point for our gaze.

One of the meditative methods used to achieve a quiet, serene mind is known as single-point concentration: that is, the ability to fix our minds on a single object to the exclusion of all others. In this way the mind becomes focused – erratic, disruptive or disturbing thoughts evaporate. Position flowers in your home with this technique in mind – meditate on them yourself to test the effects. If your mind wanders at first, gently draw it back to the flowers. Think about the subtle colours and shapes of the petals and leaves. Draw your gaze into the space in between and beyond the flowers – a space that is neither the flowers nor the background walls. It is here that your gaze is drawn inward, into your natural state of inner quietude.

ALL PHOTOGRAPHS: *Chrysanthemum indicum* 'Shamrock'

imaginary landscapes

For hundreds of years chrysanthemums have been cultivated in the Far East. As they bloom at the end of the harvest months, they have come to represent a time of repose and satisfaction when the season's work is done. In the Orient the radial arrangement of their petals is often compared to the rays of the sun, and in Japan the orderly unfolding of chrysanthemum flowers is regarded as a symbol of perfection. On this simple dining table, glass pots fade away into the background and the heads of green blooms appear to be floating in space. By taking away the dark green, ornate leaves and long stems of the flowers, the chrysanthemum heads become more central and essential. Hovering nonchalantly over crisp, white tablelinen, they seem to create their own magical winding pathway.

"Live and sleep without

worry or speculation."

Dogen

THIS PAGE AND OPPOSITE: *Muscari armeniacum*

a bedtime story

Like bedroom interiors, bedroom flowers should be relaxing in appearance as well as scent and tone; their colours cool and soothing; their shapes soft and gentle. Avoid strongly-scented flowers. Instead, for a restful night's sleep, choose plants and flowers with a mildly relaxing fragrance, such as lavender or rosemary.

Bedroom flowers are always highly personal and intended to enrich the spirit of the occupants. Arrange them with care and keep your containers and designs short, compact and stable. As you work with the flowers, keep in mind the simple image of sturdiness; the result will be kind and comforting.

instinct

designing from the heart

INSTINCT: DESIGNING FROM THE HEART

LIBERATE RATHER THAN DELIBERATE. ALL TOO OFTEN FLOWER ARRANGING CAN BECOME A STEP-BY-STEP EXERCISE. WHEN WE TRY TO CREATE AN APPEALING OR "PROPER" FLOWER DESIGN, WE SOMETIMES CONCENTRATE SO MUCH ON COMPOSITION AND TECHNIQUE THAT THE ESSENTIAL SPIRIT AND JOY OF BEING WITH FLOWERS ARE LOST ALONG THE WAY. BY ADHERING CLOSELY TO A SPECIFIC INTENTION – FOR EXAMPLE, SETTING OURSELVES THE GOAL OF CREATING A CASUAL AND CHEERFUL COMPOSITION – FROM THE VERY BEGINNING, WE LOSE THE REALITY, THE CASUAL CAREFREE SPIRIT OF THE CREATION. FROM TIME TO TIME WE NEED TO ABANDON PURPOSE AND SENSE THE FREEDOM FROM WITHIN.

IN THIS CHAPTER WE RELISH FLOWERS FOR WHAT THEY ARE AND WORK WITH THEIR NATURAL BEAUTY. INFORMALITY HOLDS SWAY AND WE GO WITH OUR INNER FEELINGS. WITH THE SAME EASY CONFIDENCE THAT WE USE TO SCRIBBLE OUR SIGNATURE, WE CAN MAKE OUR FLOWER ARRANGEMENTS DISTINCTIVE, INDIVIDUAL AND PERSONAL.

SPONTANEOUS ARRANGING OF FLOWERS WITHIN OUR INTERIORS ACHIEVES A VARIETY OF MOODS AND STATEMENTS. FLOWERS CAN BE USED TO ENHANCE AND HEIGHTEN THE ATMOSPHERE, WHETHER YOU WISH TO INTRODUCE DRAMA AND

EXCITEMENT INTO A LIVING ROOM OR CREATE A CALMING BATHROOM SANCTUARY OR BEAUTIFUL BOUDOIR. ABANDON ANY PRECONCEIVED IDEAS ABOUT YOUR INTERIORS AND LET THE FLOWERS LEAD YOU. IF YOU RELY ON YOUR INNER PERCEPTIONS, AND FOLLOW YOUR INSTINCTS RATHER THAN ANY RIGID TECHNIQUES, YOU WILL INITIATE A SENSE OF RELAXED COMFORT WHICH EXTENDS BEYOND THE FLOWERS AND ENVELOPS THE WHOLE ROOM.

THERE ARE NUMEROUS WAYS TO ARRANGE, SAY, A BUNCH OF BLUEBELLS (WILD HYACINTHS) OR DAFFODILS, YET THERE IS NO RIGHT OR WRONG APPROACH. IN THIS CHAPTER THERE ARE NO HOW-TO TIPS TO BEAR IN MIND AND NO PARTICULAR EXAMPLES TO EMULATE. THE PAGES THAT FOLLOW MERELY REFLECT THE SENSE OF JOY AND CONFIDENCE WITH WHICH THE FLORAL DESIGNS AND INTERIORS HAVE BEEN CREATED. THEY SHOW US THE BEAUTY OF HAPHAZARD ARRANGEMENTS, THE WONDER OF CHANCE FINDINGS AND THE PLEASURE TO BE DERIVED FROM NATURAL CURIOSITY. THERE ARE NO GOALS TO REACH. WITH AN OPEN HEART AND AN OPEN MIND, LET YOUR FEELINGS BE YOUR GUIDE.

country modern and urban rustic

To discover our fundamental nature, we must rely on our innate perceptions to take us to the right decisions. Relinquish the demands of society, its expectations and norms. Abandon preconceived goals, purposes, intentions and desires. Through spontaneity and freedom we can make an environment which is true to us, our origins and our place in time.

With its rustic dresser and beams, the room (below) belongs firmly to its country surroundings, yet the interior design is starkly modern. The straight, clean lines of the interior are offset by the table

ABOVE: *Salix contorta*, Wood rose OPPOSITE: *Aloe vera*

displays which show long twigs of twisted willow and instinctively "country"-style roses, as well as square tubs of short grass. The tall vase of twigs gives height to the room.

Clearly very modern, the apartment (below) belongs unequivocally to its urban setting, the sophisticated choice of modern furniture and art emphasizing its 21st-century location. At the same time the coarse, rustic terracotta pot, with its heavily grounded succulent, maintains a clear connection with the soil, as does the rough-hewn table.

LEFT (ABOVE): *Rudbeckia nitida*   LEFT (BELOW): *Rosa* 'Cardinal Hume'
OPPOSITE: Mixed vase of herbaceous flowers including *Papaver* 'Maxi' and *Solidago*

breath of nature

Not all arrangements of flowers require pre-ordained positions in our homes, nor to be precisely contrived in order to be effective. A simple gathering of rudbeckia or roses, or a mixed bouquet, arranged and placed randomly and effortlessly on any available surface can "lift" your home in subtle but effective ways. Choose flowers from the florist that instinctively strike a chord with you. There's no need to assess why – your choice might be influenced by your mood or temperament, or a long-held passion for a certain type of flower. Whatever the reason, it doesn't matter. When you arrange the flowers, let them fall naturally in the container. Don't try to force them into any particular position or direction, just let them be. Then, carry the vase of flowers around your home until you come to a place that seems just right for the arrangement – a place where positioning the flowers has the effect of brightening and enlivening the whole area or room. Arranging and placing flowers in this way can feel strangely liberating – enjoy the experience.

BELOW (LEFT): *Chrysanthemum leucanthemum, Lavendula* species BELOW (RIGHT): *Hydrangea macrophylla*

the joy of life

As we all know, flower arrangements are often created with a purpose, and this purpose is sometimes to reflect a mood or to bring to life a certain occasion. Some examples of this are the bridal bouquet or Christmas table arrangement, which convey the different senses of celebration or seasonal festivity. In these two rooms the carefree manner of the arrangements is reminiscent of the holiday spirit. While we cannot always be away from home, the spirit of vacation can still be with us if our flowers and interiors are styled in a loose and colourful way.

What makes these arrangements so full of joy is the relaxed manner in which they were put together and also the choice of informal flowers. It is almost as if the flowers have just been gathered during a casual stroll in the gardens beyond the interiors and then unceremoniously, but with generosity, cheerfulness and delight, set in a simple vessel.

LEFT: Mixed vase including *Abelia, Dicentra, Epimedium, Geranium renardii, Leucojum aestivum, Tulipa* 'Black Parrot', *Vibernum tinus*

THIS PAGE: *Delphinium cultorum* cultivar, *syringa* 'Madame Florent Stepman' OPPOSITE: *Delphinium* cultivar

"The Great Way is not difficult for
those who have no preferences."
Hui Neng

LEFT: *Scabiosa caucasica*

pure expressions

We often come across flowers that seem to need no other arrangement than to be displayed loosely in a vase or pot. Paper-thin petals of blue scabious (above) in a simple glass jar are soothing and restful – and despite their delicate appearance are long-lasting cut flowers. The naïvety and innocence of the display belie somehow the sense of youthful exuberance we get from the arrangement – perhaps they remind us of collecting and displaying country flowers as a child.

This is certainly the case with the explosion of meadow buttercups in an earthenware pot (opposite, above). Set among grasses, the buttercups instantly transport us to a time in our childhood when the golden reflection of the petals on our chin promised future wealth, a love of butter, or that we would answer a question truthfully. Meanwhile, a fountain of white irises brings a sense of sophistication to a garden table. Perfect for displaying in a courtyard or on a patio or deck, irises are great sun-lovers and a beautiful reminder that we should enjoy the sunshine while it lasts!

RIGHT [ABOVE]: *Ranunculus acris* RIGHT [BELOW]: *Iris* 'Casablanca'

ALL PHOTOGRAPHS: *Hyacinthoides non-scripta (Scilla)*

forest floor

One of the few true blue flowers in existence, the blue-bell (wild hyacinth) is, for many people, the ultimate forest flower, instinctively conjuring up in us a sense of childhood freedom and spontaneity. In the photograph (centre), bluebells are casually placed in a shallow glass container, their delicate stems unable to withstand complex or contrived arrangement.

The gently-bowing flower head reminds us that humility is a great virtue. The unassuming bluebell plant has lived on earth far longer than humankind and is a perfect emblem for the endurance of the natural world. If you go on a woodland walk, look out for bluebells – all the more beautiful for being in their natural habitat. Be very careful of the plant's leaves: try to avoid treading on them – doing so can damage the plant irrevocably.

The short-lived blooms remind us of our own transient being, while their delicate casual beauty represents the freedom within ourselves.

BELOW: *Muscari armeniacum, Narcissus* 'Canaliculatus', *Fritillaria meleagris*

FAR LEFT: *Malus floribunda* 'Golden Hornet' LEFT: *Bupleurum, Ranunculus, Tulipa* 'Apricot Parrot'

serendipity

Quirkiness is a quality often disregarded in contemporary interiors but sometimes it is simply the presence of one offbeat object that gives an interior its character and individuality. Be creative when you choose the vessels in which to display your flowers. Contemporary arrangements need not be limited to sleek vases containing a few stems of the flower of the moment. Try to achieve a sense of spontaneity by creating arrangements in vessels that are not necessarily intended for floral display – or even choose containers that seem at odds with the room in which the arrangement is to be placed. Minimal, modern rooms, for example, can accentuate the beauty of antique objects; conversely, a classical interior can enhance the lines of a modern "sculpted" vase. Allow yourself to be swayed by unpredictability when choosing a vessel for floral display, and respond to its characteristics – such as colours or patterns – as you create your arrangement.

"The shadows flee from the

face of the sun,

Who begins her restless

march of triumph."

Theodor Fontane

ALL PHOTOGRAPHS: *Helianthus annuus and decapetalus* 'Elite Sun'

sunflowers

Few flowers are as immediately evocative as the sunflower. Feelings of abundance, freedom and energy seem to pour from every golden petal. The 19th-century artist Vincent van Gogh, who suffered severe melancholy throughout his life, famously painted sunflowers, and he is said to have done so at moments of optimism and hope. A traditionally rural flower, the sunflower is usually cultivated for its oil-laden seeds.

In the interior shown above, the sunflower stems are cut close to the heads so that the flowers form a magnificent low-table arrangement. However, sunflowers (the traditional, giant variety) can grow to heights of up to ten feet (three metres) – although shorter stems are more widely available. Leaving the stems long and setting the flowers in a tall container on the floor can make a dramatic impact at an entrance or in a hallway.

THIS PAGE: *Hamamelis mollis* OPPOSITE: *Cymbidium* [orchid]

summer garden

A traditional summer bouquet is often made up of a mass of colourful garden flowers, placed symmetrically, with each type of flower distributed evenly throughout the arrangement. In the bouquet shown above (and detailed, opposite), the aim has been to capture the essence of a modern summer garden – in a vase. Since the late-20th century, garden design has become more instinctive in approach. Formal rows of many varieties of flowers have been passed over for fewer plants positioned more unexpectedly. The intention in the arrangement shown here is to capture the same spirit. Just as with the modern garden, the core themes in this bouquet are asymmetry and unexpected grouping.

A typical combination of summer garden flowers would perhaps include delphinium, lilac, guelder rose and Chinese peony. In this arrangement the tall, feathery spears of delphiniums are grouped to one side, while shorter-cut lilac and lady's mantle are deliberately massed together to accentuate the asymmetry. To avoid extreme contrasts, colours are kept subtle and the variation is tonal. The over-all effect is of a bouquet that is fresh-looking and fragrant, and one that brings all the pleasures of a modern summer garden into our homes.

OPPOSITE AND LEFT: *Alchemilla mollis*, *Delphinium cultorum* cultivars, *Syringa vulgaris* cultivars 'Herman Eilers', *Syringa vulgaris* cultivars 'Madame Florent Stepman'

OPPOSITE: *Tulipus* cultivar

picture postcard

A flower arrangement does not need to follow strict rules or guidelines. Think of arranging flowers as an attempt to create your own picture. Draw inspiration from favourite images – a ceramic dish at home, a postcard recently received from a friend travelling abroad, or your memories of the vibrant colours of an exotic spice market you visited on vacation. When these images are fresh and clear, you can enjoy recapturing them through your arrangements. Just remember always to keep it simple, and that the fewer varieties of flowers you use, the more successful you are likely to be.

While a vibrant mixed bouquet may obviously represent a bustling bazaar or a richly decorated plate, a few heads of colourful flowers can conjure up the same lively images. Like a still-life canvas, it's not always the variety of flowers that counts but how you put them together to achieve a living, moving composition.

"Inside you there is an artist

you do not know about ... Say yes

quickly, if you know, if you've

known it from before the beginning

of the universe."

Rumi

situation

responding to the room

SITUATION: RESPONDING TO THE ROOM

POETRY EXISTS IN OUR EVERYDAY LIVES. WHILE CERTAIN PRIZED OBJECTS OR POS-SESSIONS MAY ALWAYS BE REMARKABLE TO US, OUR ENTHUSIASM FOR OTHERS IS OFTEN LOST, SIMPLY BECAUSE WE BECOME OVERFAMILIAR WITH THEM. IN THE SAME WAY, WHEN AN INTERIOR OR FEATURE WITHIN A ROOM IS VIEWED ON A DAILY BASIS, THE INITIAL EXCITEMENT YOU FELT WHEN YOU FIRST WALKED INTO THE ROOM, OR WHEN YOU FIRST LAID YOUR DECORATIVE MARK ON IT, MAY DISAPPEAR. YET WE SHOULD NEVER FORGET THAT THE CHARM OF OUR SPACE STILL LURKS THERE – IT JUST NEEDS TO BE REDISCOVERED. SOMETIMES, ALL IT TAKES IS A FRESH PAIR OF EYES TO PERCEIVE BEAUTY THAT IS ABSENT FROM OUR OWN MINDS. FOR EXAMPLE, A VISITOR TO YOUR HOME MAY REMARK ON THE EXQUISITENESS OF A PAINTING, WHICH FOR YOU HAS BECOME MUNDANE.

LOST POETRY CAN BE REGAINED THROUGH NEW PERCEPTIONS. DECONTEXTUALIZING ALLOWS US TO SEE THINGS IN A DIFFERENT LIGHT. FOR EXAMPLE, IF TEN PEOPLE WERE TO STAND IN THE SAME DOORWAY AND TAKE A SNAPSHOT OF AN INTERIOR, THE RESULTS WOULD BE WIDE-RANGING. EACH OF THEM WOULD FOCUS THE FRAME OF THEIR CAMERA ON WHAT THEY CONSIDERED TO BE OF PARTICULAR INTEREST. SIMILARLY, IN INTERIOR DESIGN AND FLOWER ARRANGING, CERTAIN DETAILS CAN BE ABSTRACTED OR DEFINED SO THAT OUR VIEWPOINT SHIFTS TO A DIFFERENT ANGLE

OR FOCUS. FLOWERS ARE EXCELLENT TOOLS TO USE WHEN "REDESIGNING" ROOMS IN THIS WAY. IN THIS CHAPTER YOU WILL SEE HOW FLOWERS CAN ENHANCE A COLLECTION OF PRECIOUS FURNITURE AND ARTIFACTS AND LIFT THE WHOLE LOOK OF AN INTERIOR. OTHER EXAMPLES DEMONSTRATE THE SPATIAL AND SCULPTURAL QUALITIES OF FLOWERS. THROUGH SENSITIVE CHOICE, FRESH APPROACHES TO ARRANGING TECHNIQUES AND CAREFUL POSITIONING WITHIN A ROOM, THE EVERYDAY ASPECTS OF YOUR HOME TAKE ON NEW, INSPIRATIONAL PERSPECTIVES.

WHEN WE DISCOVER A WAY OF ARRANGING FLOWERS THAT PERFECTLY COMPLEMENTS THE STYLE OF OUR HOME, WE OFTEN TEND TO REPEAT IT – EITHER IN THE SAME KIND OF VASES OR BY PLACING ARRANGEMENTS IN SIMILAR LOCATIONS. EVERY NOW AND THEN, TAKE A LOOK AROUND YOUR HOME. REGARD IT FROM DIFFERENT ANGLES, STUDY ITS FEATURES, CONSIDER ITS ADVANTAGES AND DISADVANTAGES, AND THINK ABOUT HOW YOU CAN PLAY THESE UP OR DOWN. IMAGINE YOU ARE A VISITOR TO YOUR HOME. WHAT ARE YOUR FIRST IMPRESSIONS? ARMED WITH THIS KNOWLEDGE, YOU CAN REINVENT YOUR HOME WITH SENSITIVITY. USE FLOWERS TO CREATE YOUR OWN VISUAL LANGUAGE – THE RESULTS WILL BE DEEPLY REWARDING.

contemporary *tokonoma*

Central to the layout of traditional Japanese interiors is the concept of creating an architectural recess – a *tokonoma* – to accommodate an arrangement of flowers, a sculpture or a painting. In the contemporary loft space (shown above and opposite), a column of polished plaster creates a modern-day *tokonoma* at the junction of the stairway and landing.

Traditionally, the Japanese flower arrangements displayed in a *tokonoma* would have been "directional" – in other words, deliberately designed with their front view facing into the room. Here, the arrangement can be viewed from all directions. When this is the case, the design does not have to be complicated or elaborate. Four simple amaryllis heads point in four different directions, creating a radial arrangement that is perfectly offset by the circular vessel. The result works equally well from every angle.

OPPOSITE AND LEFT: *Hippeastrum*

precious objects

The interiors on these pages have been put together lovingly. Every object has been selected with a discerning eye. Here the unifying theme is neither colour nor style – what brings the rooms together is the uniqueness and preciousness of every object, the choice of floral display being no exception.

Extraordinary heleconia (opposite) is placed singly in an extraordinary vase. The succulent, agave (above and opposite), is a rare and exotic example of the variety. Their owner's subtle choice suggests a profound connoisseurship. The uniquely confident positioning of arrangements within these rooms enhances the air of preciousness and rarity, and connects them to the exotic and exquisite interiors.

"To be enlightened by all things is to
remove the barriers between self and others."

Dogen

OPPOSITE: *Agave victoriae-reginae* LEFT: *Agave victoriae-reginae* (left). *Heliconia pendula* (right)

OPPOSITE: *Paphiopedilum* THIS PAGE: *Anigozanthos*

ABOVE: *Aloe vera*

barren land

Arid environments are complemented by succulent varieties of plant or flower. In the interior shown here, an aloe plant suits perfectly the natural oak floorboards at the base of a modern stairwell. Low-maintenance, with their water-retaining leaves, aloe vera are extremely practical for sunny interiors, where they will thrive even with minimum care. Looking down at the plant from the top of the stairs, the broad spread of its leaves makes it the perfect plant to be viewed from above. Try to think "three-dimensionally" when placing flowers or plants within your home (for example, a single-stem flower arrangement, or a tall cactus would not have worked so well here).

Known as the "miracle plant", aloe is renowned for the healing properties of its cooling leaves – in the middle ages, the plant was thought to cast out evil spirits from the sick. Aloe has long been used to soften and beautify the skin, as well as to encourage quick healing of cuts and burns. The aloe is also reputed to enhance fertility and encourage longevity.

One of the most obvious effects of displaying flowers in our homes is to bring nature indoors, and in so doing we begin to break down the boundaries between interior and exterior. When flowers are placed in a room with a translucent boundary, the distinction between what is outside and what is inside dissolves to give us a wonderful sense of infinite space. In Japan, sliding screens (known as *shoji*) are used expressly for this purpose. In the West, glass doors or floor-to-ceiling windows have a similar effect.

However, glass walls do not always break down divisions, and in this interior (above and opposite) they may be used to create a boundary. Square panes of glass sharply separate the chaos of nature from the calm order within.

There is an interesting contrast between the wild-looking garden and the clean, distinct lines of the room emphasized by the glass walls. Within the interior, the tidy lily stems and petals complement its orderly design.

man-made nature

OPPOSITE AND ABOVE: *Zantedeschia* species and cultivars

ABOVE: *Platycerium bifurcatum* OPPOSITE: *Juncus effusus*

living sculpture

One interesting way to use plants in the home is to turn them into pieces of sculpture that work together with our interiors. The stag's-horn fern (opposite) sits on top of a tall metal "plinth". On the one hand, the height of the plinth accentuates the tall ceiling of the room, and on the other, the plinth integrates the plant into the interior – making it a companion piece to the standard lamp.

Similar sculptural effects can be obtained more simply by placing a grass (such as the corkscrew rush, shown right), or even a hardy flower (perhaps a daisy or calla lily), in a vase or pot and then transferring it to a transparent box. Filling the box with pebbles creates a plinth. As a general rule, to produce the most effective living sculpture, try to use a container with straight lines, made from simple, undecorated materials.

The room (opposite) is full of light, quiet attentiveness and modesty and is as pure a living environment as can be imagined. If you fill your rooms with clutter, your mind and spirit are similarly blocked with obstacles. The purity and clarity of this interior encourage purity and clarity to develop in the mindstream.

RIGHT: *Xanthorrhoea australis, Zantedeschia* 'Green Goddess' OPPOSITE (LEFT AND RIGHT): *Xanthorrhoea australis*

elements of surprise

Flowers spilling out from hidden corners of an interior and tall grasses disproportionate in height to the size of a table are two very different interpretations of the theme of the unexpected. Search your home for nooks and alcoves where it might not seem obvious at first to display arrangements of flowers. A precarious-looking niche in the wall of the kitchen (opposite) might seem too small for floral display, but this architectural feature presents a perfect setting for an arrangement of tall, bold flowers. On a dining table, however, we might expect to see a larger arrangement, and slender grasses in clear vases would bring a sense of vitality to a gathering of family or friends.

"If you blink your eye,

it is gone."

Mumon

"... the perceptions of the senses give news of that which is beyond their perception; they pick up hints of hidden wisdom."

Rumi

ABOVE: *Salix, Triteleia* RIGHT: *Triteleia* OPPOSITE: *Salix, Triteleia*

the perfection of flowers

The stark, clean lines of contemporary buildings can often appear too rigid. To soften the effect, architects introduce curves into their designs. In the dynamic interior (above), the architects relied on a well of natural light created by the addition of an internal courtyard. Light literally bounces off the walls and highlights the wonderful proportions of the space.

To complement the vitality of the architecture, a built-in cantilevered table was created – complete with integral glass containers – to give the illusion that the flowers are growing through the table. A perfectly-proportioned container filled with sprigs of fresh wild blossoms softens the pared-down look.

This home is a pure realization of the clear constructs of the architect's mind: organized, balanced and beautiful. By introducing the effortless perfection of the natural element, the pure, formal environment is filled with unrestricted joy, movement and life.

BELOW: *Phalaenopsis schilleriana* OPPOSITE: *Rosa* 'Cardinal Hume'

rustic monastic

In rooms with rough surfaces – thick, uneven walls, distressed furniture, heavily-textured fabrics – lightly arranged flowers bring accents of gentleness and introduce the beauty of the subtle energies of life. On these pages the blatant modernity of bare concrete has been transcended in an understated and engaging way. The bedroom (opposite) is starkly simplistic – its plain walls are almost aggressive but the inherent gentleness (a poetry akin to the rough perfection of a Japanese tea-ceremony cup) is brought out by the curve of the ceiling and by the exotic orchids sitting on the ledge. Another good way to express the natural, vital wisdom of a subtle and profound interior is to display delicate flowers in smooth vases (below).

OPPOSITE: *Lathyrus odoratus* THIS PAGE: *Salix caprea*

ABOVE: *Oncidium* (orchid) OPPOSITE: *Strelitzia reginae*

"I see your face as a sacred fire that gives

light and life to the whole universe."

Bhagavad Gita

living fire

Exotic bird-of-paradise flowers (above) are available in various tones of fiery colours, from bright yellow through burnt orange and flame red. If you have a room furnished in subtle tones, these flowers will immediately brighten the interior, adding a sense of warmth. When displaying bird-of-paradise flowers, avoid any temptation to mix them with other blooms. These striking flowers work best alone – the different colours of the petals of an individual flower head do not need further embellishment. A few green leaves will tone down their effect, if necessary.

Bright yellow orchid blossoms (opposite) bring a touch of Eastern exoticism to the interior, their gentle heads softening the cold, linear stone fireplace. These flowers glow like flames – the flickers of a gently-burning fire.

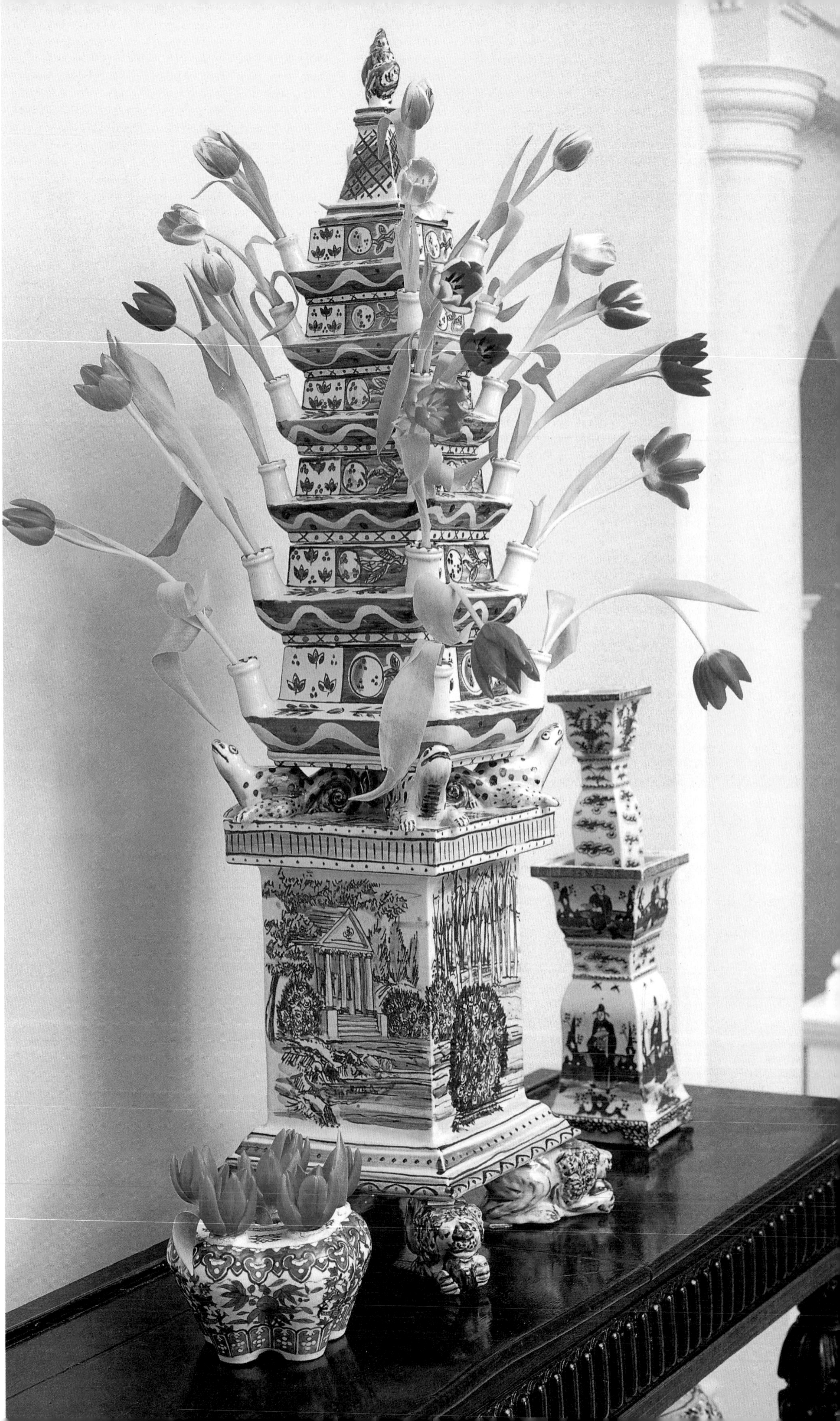

OPPOSITE AND BELOW: *Tulipa* 'Kees Nelis', 'Prominence', 'Upstar'

traditional *tulipière*

The tulip is a well-travelled flower, having originated in Asia Minor and the Mediterranean, before making its journey East into China and West into Spain (and then the rest of Europe and America). At one time the tulip was displayed in a specially-created vase known as a *tulipière*. Rarely seen nowadays, the *tulipière*'s origins lie in the 17th century when tulips were first introduced into Europe. At that time many new varieties of tulip were created through horticultural experiment. These scientific mutations were costly and soon became symbols of wealth and status, prized for their beauty and rarity. Through individual spouts designed to hold each tulip stem, the *tulipière* emphasized the preciousness of each tulip flower. The idea of the flower as a wonderful object to be admired for its beauty and individuality now reaches far beyond the tulip. It is an approach gaining in popularity in contemporary design, where sleek, narrow vessels, each created to hold a single flower stem, are used more and more often in floral display. Some effects are shown on the following pages.

modern *tulipière*

The room shown above and opposite utilizes the idea of the modern *tulipière*. In this interior the flowers are an extension of the individual vases in which they are placed, and each flower can be appreciated for its own unique beauty. Obtaining single-stem vessels need not be expensive – clear, liqueur ("shot") glasses with individual gerbera heads, cut close to the flower, or small ceramic bowls with floating gerbera or water lilies can be stunning. In this room, the effect of displaying individual tulips in a row on the coffee table is to bring a sense of organization and regularity to the elegant, but otherwise lively room, and to provide a central focus for the seating around the table.

"For we are lovers of the beautiful,

yet simple in our tastes."

Pericles

OPPOSITE AND RIGHT: *Tulipa* 'Rococo'

harmonized space

When arranging flowers in a room it is important to think about how their position – their situation in the room – will affect the overall space. On these pages we see how the same flower, arranged differently, creates a completely different sense of an interior. Placed beneath a painting, the arrangement of brightly-coloured gerberas (opposite) becomes the foremost focal point. Their vibrant colours resemble those used in the artist's painting and the arrangement becomes a gallery artwork in itself. Above left, a low arrangement of red gerberas achieves harmony and formal balance, while a single gerbera stem in a plain glass vessel (above right) is used to convey modesty and simplicity.

ALL PHOTOGRAPHS: *Gerbera jamesonii*

RIGHT: *Populus tremula*

contrasting lines

It is unusual for an architect to integrate nature into the very fabric of a building design as surely as he or she introduces a concrete pillar. Yet here, glass walls have been designed to act almost like cinema screens onto which silhouettes of trees and plants are projected by the natural light. Still more unusual are the arrangements of twigs twisting naturally into seemingly random lines, unlike the linear design of the building.

At its most abstract, architecture means the careful placement of complementary lines, colours and shapes. This interior is a deliberate collection of rigid lines. Although the arrangements appear to be in complete contrast, the introduction of a natural free-flowing element emphasizes the strength of the man-made architecture. The sheer perfection of the structure's lines is echoed in the slenderness of the twigs.

postmodernism

ABOVE: *Cupressus macrocarpa* 'Goldcrest'

Postmodernism is an abstract language, characterized by the use of pure shapes such as cones, cubes and spheres. The Postmodernist movement challenged the way we view architecture and design, and treated contrasting colours as flat, geometric shapes superimposed one on top of the other. Shapes and colours did not suggest or relate to one another but instead, remained as disjointed elements in a composition.

Similarly, in the hallway (above) the distinctive "flowers" are formed of feathers, and geometric shapes on the curved table (opposite) are echoed in the evergreen set in a cube-shaped planter. In each interior, the elements remain abstract and disassociated. At the very least, this method of deconstructing flowers and plants offers surprise; at best, it challenges our preconceptions and our understanding of arrangement.

ABOVE: *Lilium* 'Centurion' OPPOSITE: *Malus*

falling waters

Perhaps more than any other private residence in the world, Falling Waters (opposite) – designed by architect Frank Lloyd Wright (1867–1959) – epitomizes how modern architecture can integrate with nature. The building is not an attempt to become part of nature, nor to simply open up vistas upon nature. Wright acknowledged the inevitable distinctness of the building from its surroundings. The greatness of Falling Waters is that it integrates on a very subtle level with the spirit of nature. Interior and exterior are infused with the underlying harmony of the surrounding natural world.

To help us to reach and understand this conclusion, Wright used a series of pointers in his design. The natural flagstone floor, the wooden furniture and colourful fabrics all suggest the outdoors. Through clever vision, the natural poetry of outdoors has been recreated indoors. Of course the choice of flowers and plants for the interior of the building are much more specific to the exterior, although, paradoxically, they offer no direct visual contact with the landscape immediately visible beyond the large expanses of glass. This venerated building goes beyond design and into the spirit of nature. Falling Waters is not a building – it is sorcery and poetry in stone and concrete.

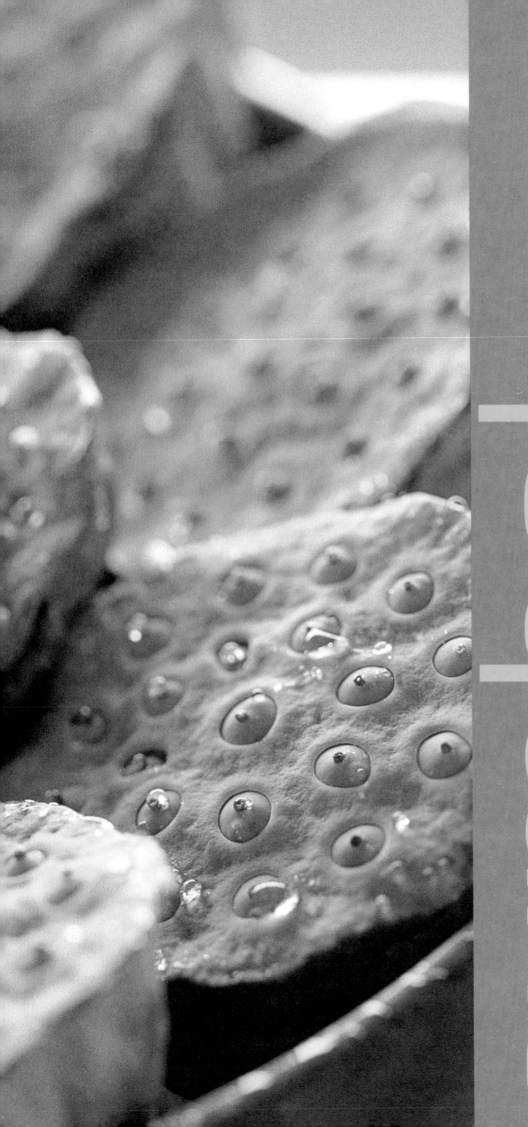

symbol

designing beyond design

SYMBOL: DESIGNING BEYOND DESIGN

THERE COMES A POINT WHEN DESIGN CEASES TO BE PURELY A SKILL OR AN ACCOMPLISHMENT, OR TO BE BASED ON A CERTAIN SET OF RULES OR PRINCIPLES. IT BECOMES A PART OF US: A METAPHOR FOR THE WAY WE ARE AND THE WAY WE DO THINGS. THE MOVE BEYOND DESIGN DOES NOT TAKE YEARS OF EXPERIENCE TO BUILD UP, JUST CONFIDENCE AND SELF-REALIZATION. MANY OF THE ARRANGEMENTS IN THIS CHAPTER ARE SIMPLE TO RECREATE. WE DO NOT NEED TO LEARN ANYTHING NEW, JUST REDISCOVER THE INNER POOL OF CREATIVITY AND STILLNESS WITH WHICH WE ARE ALL BORN. A TRANSFORMATION OR SHIFT OCCURS IN OUR RESPONSE TO FLORAL DISPLAY WHEN WE STOP FORCING OURSELVES TO ARRANGE WITH PURITY, QUIET ATTENTIVENESS AND INSIGHT, AND WE REALIZE THAT THESE QUALITIES ARE ALREADY PRESENT WITHIN US – HAVE ALWAYS BEEN THE FUNDAMENTAL PART OF US – AND SO AUTOMATICALLY GO INTO ANY ARRANGEMENT WE CHOOSE TO CREATE.

THIS TRANSFORMATION IS NOT UNIQUE TO DESIGN – IT CAN HAPPEN AT ANY MOMENT IN ALMOST ANY KIND OF ACTIVITY. ALL THAT IS NEEDED IS AWARENESS. THE ZEN-NESS OF THE VERTICAL DISPLAY ON PAGES 164–5 IS A GOOD EXAMPLE OF HOW FLORAL DESIGN DISPLAYS OUR INHERENT QUALITIES: PURITY, SIMPLICITY AND SERENITY. ONCE WE REDISCOVER THESE ATTRIBUTES DEEP WITHIN, WE CAN ARRANGE EFFORTLESSLY, AND WITHOUT ANY SENSE OF FORCED CREATIVITY OR

FRUSTRATION. THE RESULT OF ALL THIS IS A PROFOUND SENSE OF PEACE, HARMONY AND BALANCE, REFLECTED IN OUR ARRANGEMENTS.

BUT IF AN ARRANGEMENT OF FLOWERS IS A REFLECTION (A SYMBOL) OF OUR OWN TRUE NATURE, THEN THE FLOWERS THEMSELVES MUST HAVE THEIR OWN VOICE. ALSO IN THIS CHAPTER WE LOOK AT SOME OF THE MEANINGS OF FLOWERS, AND HOW THOSE MEANINGS CAN BE USED TO REFLECT OTHER ESSENTIAL ASPECTS OF THE SELF. THE TAOIST ELEMENTS, FOR EXAMPLE, ARE ABSTRACT CONCEPTS PRESENT IN EVERYTHING FROM OUR HOMES TO OUR OWN PHYSICAL AND SPIRITUAL MAKE-UP. BY USING FLOWERS TO BALANCE THESE ELEMENTS, WE CREATE SPACE FOR MORE HARMONIOUS AND TRANQUIL LIVING. SIMILARLY, THE SYMBOLISM OF A SINGLE FLOWER HEAD OR THE COLOUR OF ITS PETALS CAN BE CHOSEN WITH THE EXPRESS PURPOSE OF REMINDING US OF SOME OF THE SIMPLEST, MOST PERFECT SUBTLETIES IN LIFE – AMONG THEM, PURITY, INNOCENCE, KINDNESS, HUMILITY AND TRANQUILLITY.

rationality and mysticism in colour

Flowers have a mystical side which stems from the sometimes profound associations we have already made about their colour and form. Our home is a vehicle for self-expression and our choice of flowers reflects this. Primary colours evoke symmetry, energy and clarity, and it is by no means accidental that the Modernist movement (which valued these three qualities) embraced the colours of blue, yellow and red. Muted earth colours, however, have more esoteric associations, such as fertility rituals and mysticism. In some tribal societies certain earth colours relate to the spirit world.

The same mix of rationality and mysticism can also be expressed through flowers. Flowers in muted colours (left) are a harmonious continuation of the esoteric, slightly mystical approach of the designer. The vivid blue of the irises in a predominantly rational, modernist interior (right) is consistent with the classically-shaped terracotta pot in the background. Both of these interiors demonstrate two diametrically opposing, yet internally coherent, examples of how colour, flowers and interiors can be brought together.

OPPOSITE: *Chrysanthemum* ABOVE: *Iris* 'Professor Blaauw'

the vertical zen garden

While some arrangements draw upon the specific symbolism of the flowers they use, others, in just a few stems, capture the spirit of an entire tradition. These cyperus stems (known variously as the umbrella plant or crown palm) set against a backdrop of muted light are immediately reminiscent of Zen Buddhism. A certain contrived austerity reminds us of the thoughtful creation of the Zen garden. In this interior the Japanese courtyard of pure gravel has been replaced by large, white semitransparent linen blinds. Against this empty field, shadows and tall, clear stems of cyperus draw meditative, serene lines like raked gravel.

The Noguchi Akari horn lamp replaces the focal point of the Zen garden – a carefully positioned natural rock. Noguchi was famous for his rock sculptures. Interestingly, he also produced some of the best modern interpretations of the Zen garden. In this pared-down composition the heavy lamp is balanced by light cyperus. Simple, yet discerning, the arrangement retains the tranquil and peaceful spirit which is Zen.

OPPOSITE AND LEFT: *Cyperus alternifolius*

"Zen teaches us ... to understand
that the truth of the universe is
ultimately our own true self."

Seung Sah

calligraphy

One of the most emblematic features of Eastern cultures is the beautiful calligraphic writing. While the interiors displaying the floral designs on these pages are Western, both of these rooms evoke a distinct sense of the East. The stems of the flowers appear like strokes of a calligraphy brush, either in air (opposite) or on the wall (above). Opposite, the room display features an antique Chinese altar table, on which are placed brush-holders carved from bamboo.

The flowers (above) are reduced and, at the same time, elevated to bold, calligraphic strokes: confident and without regret, free of distractions and obstructions. Like shadows cast across a pool of still water, or the reflections of the moon in water-drops suspended from blades of grass, or the black earth itself, they are naturally effortless. The calligraphic quality of the arrangement projects onto the wall to become an independent, flat work of art, drawn with shadow and light on an empty wall. Our eyes are drawn to the flat form of the silhouette, where we find peace, tranquillity and a momentary end to our suffering.

BELOW: *Cynara scolymus*

"That which has no form creates form.
That which has no existence brings
things into existence."

Rumi

the empty canvas

White walls – *de rigueur* in all contemporary interiors – provide the perfect backdrop for a flower
arrangement. A white wall is like an empty
canvas – it is charged with meaning, unformed
and pure. Lucio Fontana (1899–1968), the
20th-century Italian artist, slashed through his
empty canvas, exposing the true emptiness within: turning surface into depth and depth into
surface. A flower – placed in front of a blank
white wall – affects us in much the same way.
It reminds us of the emptiness of the wall and,
by contrasting with it, exposes our relationship
with the infinite. Within our confined white
spaces, flowers are our windows. Not merely
windows to nature, flowers in a vase become
abstract lines, colour and light. And like a
vortex, they draw us beyond their form, beyond
the empty wall, and into a silent, still pool – an
inner spring of infinite knowledge.

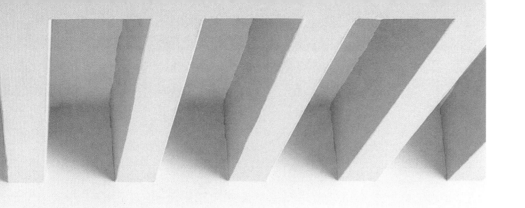

OPPOSITE AND LEFT: *Hydrangea macrophylla*

natural collage

One of the fundamental points about symbolism is that it is a system of display in which the essence of a subject is presented in a simplistic form. In modern life we have a tendency to experience only the truly extraordinary – the power of subtlety and simplicity often completely passes us by. With flowers (which embody so much symbolism), we can bring this appreciation for simplicity back into our lives by superimposing disparate ordinary elements onto each other to emphasize their true and extraordinary nature. Natural "frames" hold the contradictory elements together. For example, exotic tropical flowers and leaves set against a backdrop of wood panelling in a log cabin (opposite) are a deliberate contradiction: the two elements emphasize each other. The regular lines of the panels tame the reaching alocasia leaf. A similar effect is achieved with heads of allium set against a wooden-slatted screen (right, below).

The woven wooden screen (right, above) is a perfect backdrop for an arrangement of orchids and discarded birds' nests. In Chinese painting, a vase of orchids denotes concordance between parties, and this meaning is emphasized by the regular pattern of the weaving in the "frame". (Of course, the symbolism also makes this display perfect for a table-top – around which people may gather for discussion or negotiation.)

OPPOSITE (ABOVE): *Phalaenopsis amabilis* OPPOSITE (BELOW): *Allium* BELOW: *Alocasia, Eichhorina crassipes*

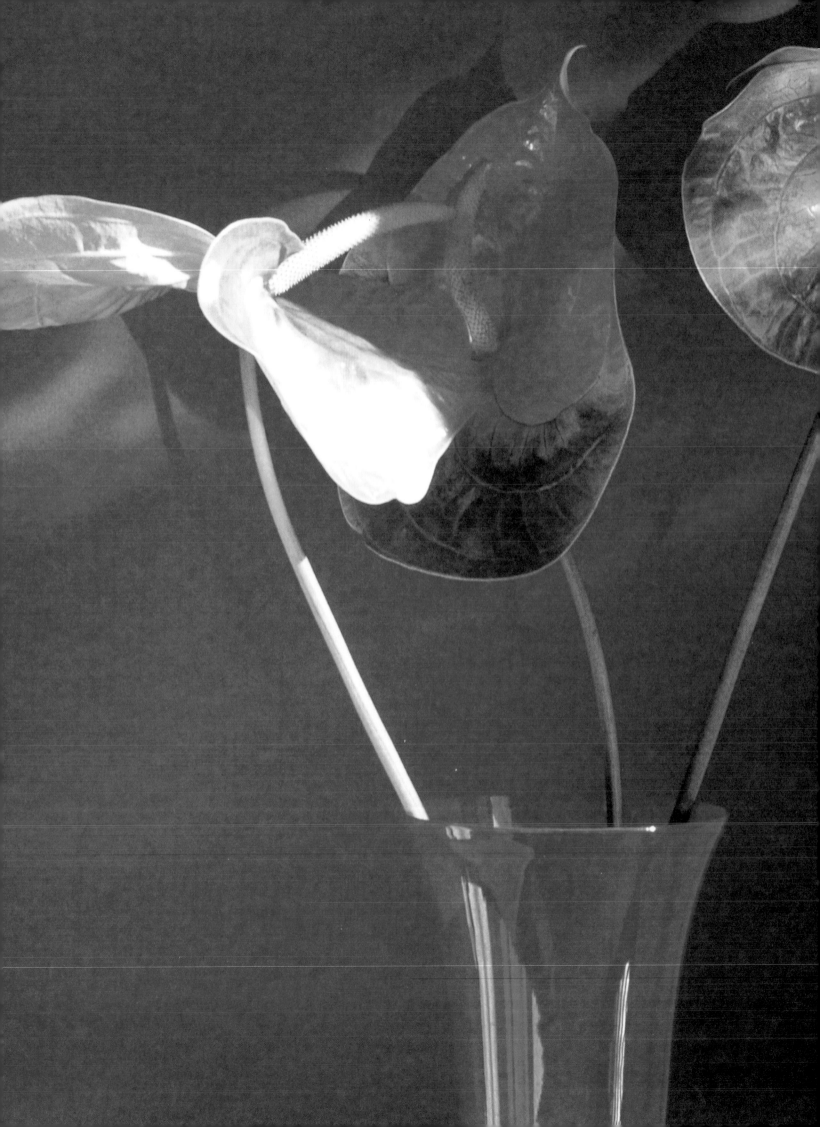

OPPOSITE: *Anthurium andraeanum* 'Paradiso' BELOW: *Paeonia*

"Be really whole
And all things will come to you."
Lao Tzu

the five elements: wood

A symbol of spring and the sunrise in the East, Wood can be displayed in our homes through the use of twigs of blossom. Simple arrangements, such as that opposite, are easy to maintain and long-lasting. Woody green stems topped with delicate buds represent wood and remind us of new life. Quince blossom echoes the Eastern design of the cabinet (the quince is a fruit native to western Asia). The Japanese lacquered chest (above) is inlaid with a ceramic depiction of the four seasons. Visible are the cherry blossom (spring), peony (summer) and chrysanthemum (fall). The effect of the design is similar to the display of blossom, reminding us of the renewal of life.

According to the principles of Feng Shui, the propitious nature of the element Wood is brought into the home through the introduction of tall columns and the colour green. Wooden furniture – or bare wooden floorboards – also evoke the power of Wood. To effect a change in your life, try to stimulate Wood energy in your home. Introduce houseplants of any kind into every room. Wood is controlled by Metal. To control Wood in your home, introduce white and silver, and avoid brightly coloured flowers or walls.

the five elements: earth

OPPOSITE AND LEFT: *Zantedeschia rehmannii*

Universally, Earth is the element that represents fecundity and protection. The colours used in the interior (opposite) – beiges, browns and yellows – immediately bring to mind the natural colours of soil itself. The square coffee table reminds us that in Taoism, Earth is graphically drawn as a square and, like a vase, it is a symbol of support and of being held. Soft floor cushions evoke this sense of protection. Earth is a centring element and in Feng Shui (the traditional Chinese art of placement), fresh flowers (here zantedeschia) displayed in the centre of the home are believed to promote a feeling of being centred and balanced in the self. When the Earth element is harmonized in our living environment, its nourishing powers unite to promote health and stability for all occupants. The beautiful funnels of the flowers, created by the curling of a single petal, remind us of abundance, fertility and nurturing.

178 **symbol**

RIGHT (ABOVE) AND OPPOSITE: *Eryngium alpinum*

the five elements: metal

Metal represents purification. We see this view reflected in theories of interior design where metal is often most closely associated with minimalism. In a minimalist environment, interiors are stripped of ornamentation and other trappings to create a mood that connects us with the pure essence of things. In Feng Shui it is said that, when the Metal element is deficient in our environment, we will find a tendency within ourselves to hang onto superfluous possessions, styles, emotions, relationships and so on. Yet when Metal is in excess, we become too rigid and judgmental of ourselves and others, and too detached from our environment.

Flowers present the perfect opportunity to balance the element of Metal within our interiors. When Metal is deficient, add white ceramic or metal vases, preferably filled with "rounded" flowers, such as purple thistles (above and opposite). Also, use flowers or foliage that – like the metal blade of a sword – have associations with elimination or separation – for example, flowers with pointed heads and leaves. Alternatively, counteract an excess of Metal by adding flowers in bright colours, with eccentric forms and interesting textures, such as red gerberas.

the five elements: water

The Water element is characterized by its dreamy formlessness. Within Water lies the potential for creativity and activity; a place where anything can happen. Water represents our inner sense of an eternal continuity beyond our temporary self, our sense of being part of a whole, where the individuated self merges with the infinity of being. The Water element symbolizes absolute rest, tranquillity and peace. It allows us to step outside ourselves. Water represents the time we take for ourselves, healing time away from our busy lives. Cool blues and black are the colours of Water. Its form is the curvaceous meandering line of a natural stream. Quiet movement, the essence of Water, can be indicated in an interior through uneven surfaces such as stone, or textured walls and rugs.

Flowers connect us to Water. In floral display this sense can be emphasized in two primary ways. Place flowers in vases of clear glass so that the water is as much a part of the arrangement as the flowers. On these pages, the flower, vase and water become integral and equal parts of the display. Water lilies have been used to further enhance the symbolism of the water (the water lily – or lotus flower – is an Eastern symbol of the source of all life). Their gently curving stems remind us of the smooth, undulating flow of water free to run its natural course. When arranging flowers, adopt a reflective sense of the infinite within and allow this to be present in your arrangement.

OPPOSITE AND LEFT: *Nymphaea capensis*

182

RIGHT [BELOW]: *Tulipa 'Yokohama'* RIGHT [ABOVE] AND OPPOSITE: *Papaver nudicale*

the five elements: fire

Fire is a symbol of divine energy, transcendence and spiritual revelation. At once destructive and creative, Fire represents the energy of the sun and is therefore one of the most important symbols in the Chinese tradition. In Feng Shui a balanced Fire element in the home can bring joy, excitement and sexual desire. However, the Fire element must be carefully controlled – too much may lead to hyperactivity, restlessness, anxiety and over-stimulation.

Flowers in warm colours – reds, pinks, peaches and vibrant oranges – are good ways to stimulate the Fire element in our interiors, and instantly bring warmth to a cold room. Try arranging them to echo the reaching tongues of bright flames (as shown with the yellow tulips, opposite). In the bedroom, red flowers simulate Fire's warming love. As Fire has a tendency to rage out of control, use red flowers carefully and in small quantities. If red alone is too intense for you, try combining it with warming orange. Red and orange poppies, with their gently curving stems, will create a sense of a softly burning hearth.

THIS PAGE: *Cyperus alternifolius* OPPOSITE: *Cocos nucifera*

flower circles

The circle is one of humankind's most ancient symbols. Among the many meanings attributed to it are unity, the passing of time and spiritual journeying. A perfect circle evokes balance and inner quiet. Exotic and striking, in one sense the anthurium is probably not the first plant we might think of to recreate an atmosphere of understated calm. Yet in this interior the carefully-contrived circular arrangement achieves just that.

Looking at this arrangement, our gaze silently flows in circles through the space and our mind follows that gaze. Our thoughts fail to halt, fix and stagnate – colours blend into colours, and matter into light. At the centre, the arrangement draws us in, centring and quietening the mind. The effect is almost hypnotic. We are reminded of a Tibetan *mandala* (an instrument of meditation). We stare into the quiet emptiness and lose ourselves within. This arrangement is symbolic without symbolizing anything – it is a circular gateway, a portal to our being.

OPPOSITE: *Anthurium andraeanum* 'Choco' and 'Midori' LEFT: *Anthurium andraeanum* 'Midori'

ABOVE (left to right): *Polianthes tuberosa, Ficus benjamina, Lilium* 'Casa Blanca' OPPOSITE (ABOVE): *Galanthus nivalis* OPPOSITE (BELOW): *Jasminum*

being at peace

Flower symbolism alludes to deeply spiritual ideas and it seems natural that certain colours, shapes and compositions of flowers will invoke various states of mind within us. By placing a single flower or an arrangement of flowers in our home, we are able to produce and convey certain feelings or moods.

Opposite, flowers surround a Buddha sculpture and echo the Buddha's qualities – liberation from suffering, as well as purity, serenity and modesty. The lily symbolizes purity and rebirth, while the fig is a symbol of moral teaching – it is the variety of tree under which the Buddha received enlightenment (known as the Bodhi tree). Like the Buddha, the rose is a symbol of unconditional love. Altogether, there is a deep sense of peace in this interior.

However, we do not need such perfect connections, or even a Buddha statue, to bring the same virtues into our homes. The snowdrop (above) is a wonderfully evocative flower. This delicate bloom displays a profound strength as it pushes its way up through frozen ground and is the first sign of renewed life following the barrenness of winter. A humble flower with such determination is surely inspirational.

Most white flowers symbolize aspects of purity: jasmine (left) represents virginity, honesty and kindness.

reference

care and conditioning of cut flowers and plants

CARE AND CONDITIONING OF CUT FLOWERS AND PLANTS

Knowing how to care for your plants and keep them healthy is the secret to creating magnificent floral displays. Whether you are buying flowers from a florist or gathering them from your own garden, it is important that you follow a few simple principles on their care and conditioning.

In this book, the term "cut flower" is used to refer to any part of a plant that has decorative value when cut. Included are not only flowers, but also foliage, leaves that resemble flowers, seed-heads and even vegetables. Outlined on the following pages are guidelines on how to prepare the plants and flowers featured in the book.

Cutting equipment

Many people cut stems with scissors or secateurs but a sharp knife is the most effective tool – it minimizes damage to the plant because it does not squeeze the stem and so rupture the water-absorbing cells. Cutting tools should always be sharp because blunt knives or scissors can easily tear the stems.

Cutting and buying times

Ideally, flowers should be cut from the garden in the early morning or in the evening. These are the coolest times of day when plants are at their healthiest – during the heat of the day, plants lose water through evaporation (or transpiration). Similarly, it is best not to buy flowers during the hottest part of the day, unless they can be immediately kept in water. Avoid leaving flowers in hot places (for example, a car) for any length of time as this can reduce their vase life by up to fifty percent.

Containers and the production of bacteria

It is essential that containers are spotlessly clean before use. This will prevent the production of bacteria (which will restrict the plant's vase life) in the flower water. Rinsing a container is not adequate – wash it thoroughly, using a scrubbing brush to remove any residue from around the rim or the base.

Cut flowers and leaves are also badly affected by decaying plant material in the water. Not only does this look unsightly, but it also contributes to the formation of bacteria and algae, which block the stem's cells and vessels, preventing the uptake of water and nutrients – in these conditions, buds and half-open flowers will not develop fully, and flowers and leaves will become flaccid and wilt prematurely.

To prevent this happening, before placing the flowers in a container, always strip off any foliage or damaged petals from the part of the stem that will fall below the water line. This will help to keep the water clean and the flowers strong and healthy.

Cutting and initial conditioning of stems

Before displaying flowers, remove the lower leaves and any damaged petals (see above). Always re-cut the stem ends. Cut about 25 mm (1 in) off each stem end. This is best done under water in a deep bucket or bowl, to prevent air locks forming. Air locks will restrict the free flow of water and nutrients up the stem. Stems should be cut at an angle to expose a large surface-area which will allow for the maximum absorption of water.

Leave flowers and leaves to condition in tepid water for at least two hours in a cool place before using them. This will extend their vase life by permitting the stems to take up the maximum amount of water possible, enabling the cells to become turgid. The plant material should be transferred immediately to the display container while the stem end is wet, so that air locks do not form.

Special stem conditioning methods

Different types of stem have different methods for conducting water and nutrients through the plant vessels. As a result special conditioning techniques that might be appropriate for one plant may not be appropriate for another, and a variety of treatments may be required when preparing different stems for display. Over the following pages, we have given information on the various treatments that can be used to encourage maximum water absorption in different types of stems.

Tepid or warm water treatment: soft and firm stems

Both soft- and firm-stemmed flowers and plants benefit greatly from conditioning with warm or tepid water before they are displayed. Warm water contains very few air bubbles, which means that it can be rapidly absorbed by the plant; the possibility of air locks forming in the stem – preventing the free flow of water up the stem and causing the flower head to wilt prematurely – is greatly reduced.

Soft-stemmed flowers which respond well to this treatment include: alstromeria, anemone, gerbera and most flowers which bloom in the springtime – for example, tulips, muscari and chincherinchees. Warm water treatment is not appropriate for daffodils, which exude a sticky sap – these should be conditioned using the searing or singeing treatment (see page 194). Firm-stemmed flowers include: carnations, several cut-flower orchids, chrysanthemums, amaranthus and a range of herbaceous flowers – for example, the michaelmas daisy. The warm water method is also very effective for dry-pack flowers (bought flowers that have not been stored in water), exotic flowers and those in tight bud.

Fill a bucket or wide-based container with about 75 mm (3 in) of warm, not boiling, water. The ideal temperature is between 35°C and 40°C (95°F and 104°F). Test the water with your hand – if it is too hot to touch, then it will be too hot for the flowers. Re-cut the stems with a sharp knife at an angle and allow them to stand in this water for about five minutes. Re-fill the bucket with cold water until the temperature is tepid and leave the flowers to condition in this tepid water for up to 2 hours before displaying. Adding plant food to the water can significantly aid the flowers' development.

Hot water treatment: woody stems

Woody-stemmed plants that benefit from hot water treatment include outdoor-grown chrysanthemums, herbaceous flowers, such as michaelmas daisies, and most trees and shrubs. The hot water opens the cells at the bottom of each stem, allowing water to pass through the stem more easily. It is essential to take great care (of yourself) when using this method as it involves boiling water. Also, before proceeding, make sure the flower heads and foliage are well protected with tissue paper or something similar – this will prevent any damage to the flowers as the steam rises up from the water.

Fill a bucket or wide-based container with about 25 to 50 mm (1 to 2 in) of boiling water. Re-cut the stem ends with a sharp knife at a long, oblique angle and plunge them immediately into the water. Leave them there for up to one minute. Then, pour cold water into the container until the water is tepid. Leave the stems to condition in the water in a cool place, out of direct heat, for up to two hours. Plant food suitable for woody stems can be added to the water.

Filling and plugging: hollow stems

Hollow-stemmed flowers, such as delphiniums, lupins and dahlias, often have difficulty taking up water after their stems have been cut. A highly effective but somewhat time-consuming method of promoting water uptake in these stems is to fill and plug them.

Hold the stem upside-down and fill it with water. Plug the end of the stem with cotton wool (absorbent cotton) or tissue (or with anything that will act as a wick). Turn the stem the right way up and place it in 150 to 200 mm (6 to 8 in) of tepid water to condition the stems.

Searing or singeing treatment: latex-producing stems

Several plants (including euphorbias, poppies and rubber plants) produce a milky or latex-type sap (which can cause an allergic reaction in some people – wearing gloves when handling the stems will help to prevent a reaction occurring). This sap can damage other plants in the display and can also contaminate the water, making it look cloudy. To prevent this, use either the hot water treatment (described left) or searing (or singeing) treatment, where the end of the stem is passed quickly over a flame. Make sure that the whole stem end is seared and then immediately place it in fairly deep tepid water for about 2 hours. Searing prevents the sap coming out and also helps to firm up the stem.

Displaying without water

In this book you will find examples of arrangements in which the flowers have been laid across bowls and other containers, and are therefore displayed out of water. Some flowers are better able to survive under

significantly increase their transpiration rate (or the rate at which water-vapour is released through their stomata). This causes petals and leaves to dry out and flowers to die prematurely. To avoid this, place your displays well away from sources of direct heat, such as radiators and sunlight.

Many plants are susceptible to the effects of ethylene gas. Ethylene is a natural plant hormone produced by plants, flowers, leaves and fruit as they age (it is also present in car exhaust fumes and cigarette smoke). The gas is odourless and is released by the plant into the air. When a plant or flower is damaged or stressed, the amount of gas produced can increase. Production also increases in the latter stages of a plant's life, speeding up the ageing process.

In the case of cut flowers, the largest amount of the gas is developed in the calyx – the part of the flower below the petals that helps to protect the bud before the flower opens and which will later form the seed box. The rate at which a flower will naturally produce ethylene is a good indicator of its vase-life qualities: some flowers are more susceptible to the gas than others. When certain fruit (such as bananas) and susceptible flowers (such as carnations) are put together in a room, the effects can be dramatic – flowers can wither and age overnight.

Other effects of this gas on the plant are yellowing and dropping of the leaves and the inability of buds to

these conditions than others, especially if they are conditioned properly first.

Calla lilies will last out of water for between 7 and 10 days if the stem ends are treated with a product called cold glue. This substance completely seals the end of the stem, allowing the plant to use the water already present in its stem. It also prevents any air from getting in and thus reduces transpiration, and the evaporation of water from the stem. This glue is available from specialist florists and some garden centres.

Harmful environments

To gain the maximum vase life out of your flowers, it is extremely important to place them in an environment in which they will be able to thrive. No matter how thoroughly and efficiently you prepare your flowers, displaying them under harmful conditions will dramatically reduce their lifespan.

The hot, dry atmosphere often found in the home can be very damaging to cut flowers and plants and may mature. To gain the maximum vase life out of your flowers, it is worth remembering to avoid leaving ripening fruit and fresh flowers together in the same room.

Ethylene-sensitive flowers include sweet peas, most species of carnations, freesias, alstroemerias and roses. Before they reach the shops, many commercial growers now pre-treat flowers to slow down their production of ethylene. These flowers can last up to fifty or sixty percent longer in the vase than non-treated stems.

GENERAL CARE OF GROWING PLANTS

The information that follows will help you gain pleasure and maximum value from your houseplants. The requirements of many plants are quite simple and are similar to our own needs: water, right temperature, light and food.

The term "houseplant" is misleading: no plant naturally grows inside a house. We have to remember that a plant develops and grows, and (unlike an ornament!) it needs certain conditions to survive. Although you may have earmarked a certain spot for a certain plant, check that the conditions of your chosen position are suited to the plant's needs. If the conditions aren't right, leaves will drop off and the plant will not thrive. However, by finding conditions within a building that fulfil as closely as possible the needs of a particular species, a large number of plants become suitable for indoor use.

There are two main ways in which to choose a houseplant: by preference of species or by position. Either select a plant you like and place it in a position where the greatest number of its needs are met, or decide on a particular place in the home where you wish to display a plant, and then select a plant that will most readily tolerate those conditions. Both these ways of selecting plants will help your plants to remain in the best condition, growing and developing for as long as possible.

As with cut flowers, a vast, worldwide, houseplant industry has emerged in recent years. This, along with vast improvements in modern propagating techniques, has meant that a tremendous variety of plants, including apparently unusual ones, are now readily available for home use. As a result, more easily than ever before we are able to choose the right plant for the right place in our home. Once the choice is made and the plant is potted and positioned, it is important to follow a few simple principles on caring for the plant to enable it to grow and develop for its whole natural life.

Watering

More house plants are killed by over-watering than anything else. Nevertheless, it is also important not to starve plants of water. The easiest way to find the right balance is to test the water content of the soil by pushing one finger into the top 30–35 mm (approximately 1–1½ in) of the compost. If the soil feels moist, do not water the plant; if it feels dry, thoroughly soak the compost, then leave the plant until the top of the soil is dry again. Then repeat the process in three to seven days.

Special rules apply to orchids. Although many orchid plants are easy to look after, they should not be left standing in water or in soaked compost – they are epiphytes (plants that have aerial roots) and need air around the roots in order to survive.

Lighting

Although we may consider a room "well lit", it may be insufficient for many plants. For basic growing condi-

will not tolerate low temperatures. However, a plant from the temperate zones will become leggy and weak in high temperatures. Having at least a rough idea of the temperature of rooms and spaces will help when selecting a plant suitable for the conditions. Many houseplants come from the tropical or sub-tropical climates of the world and will tolerate temperatures between about 15°C and 25°C (approximately 60°F and 75°F). Most plants have difficulty in tolerating great fluctuations in temperature, particularly changes between the temperatures of day and night. Placing plants in rooms where the temperature tends to be fairly constant will prolong their lives.

Avoid exposing plants to draughts: do not place them close to external doors, or windows, particularly if these doors and windows are in constant use.

Humidity

Humidity is often overlooked when we think about the optimum conditions for a houseplant. As we have said, houseplants tend to come from tropical or sub-tropical climates, many of which have high levels of humidity. The result is that plants will often thrive in our bathrooms and kitchens, where there is usually high humidity.

Feeding

As a plant thrives and grows it will need a constant supply of nutrients. Initially, the plant will extract these nutrients from the compost in which it is growing. But after a time the nutrients will be used up and a new supply will be required if the plant is to thrive. As a result, we recommend that you feed your houseplants regularly – approximately once every two weeks – with a proprietary nutrient-balanced plant food.

tions, most plants need a minimum of 500 to 800 lux – much higher if they are to thrive. As a guide, on a sunny day, a room with an average amount of natural light will have about 800 lux within about 1 metre (approximately 3 ft) of the window, dropping to 500 to 600 lux within 2 metres (about 6 ft) of the window. Try to place your plants as close as possible to natural light sources. West-facing windows will tend to let in more light than north- or east-facing windows. However, direct sunlight – for example, from a south-facing window or a conservatory, can scorch plants and burn the leaves.

Temperatures

To enjoy healthy plants, it is important to take into consideration the temperature range a plant will tolerate. If the natural habitat of a plant species is tropical, then it

GLOSSARY OF CUT FLOWERS AND PLANTS

This glossary is ordered alphabetically by botanical name (common name in CAPITALS) and gives guidelines for the buying and care of the flowers and plants featured in the book. For detailed information on the stem conditioning treatments referred to in this section, see: for tepid or warm water treatment, page 193; for hot water treatment, page 194; for filling and plugging, page 194; for searing or singeing treatment, page 194.

Abelia
ABELIA

Buy when buds are starting to open. Responds to hot water treatment. Benefits from cut-flower food for woody stems. Lasts up to 7 days in clean water.

Agapanthus africanus and Agapanthus umbellatus
AFRICAN LILY OR LILY OF THE NILE (Blue: **'Blue Triumphator'**; white: **'Alba'**)

Buy when about one-third of buds are opening. Buds and open flowers tend to drop, but feeding with flower food and regular re-cutting of stem ends will help minimize the problem. Buds take 4 to 6 days to open; full flowers last 7 to 10 days.

Alchemilla mollis
LADY'S MANTLE

Buy when flowers have just opened. Responds well to tepid water treatment. Lasts up to 7 days.

Allium species
ALLIUM OR ORNAMENTAL ONION

Buy when one-third of the flowers are open. Keep water bacteria-free (see page 192) and change regularly. Lasts up to 2 weeks.

Alocasia
ELEPHANT'S EAR

Buy when leaf looks fresh and firm, and not yellow or dry around the edges. A tropical leaf that needs to be kept in moist, humid atmosphere at about 12°C to 15°C (54°F to 59°F). Condition in tepid water. Mist to ensure moisture and humidity. Keep away from direct heat. Lasts up to 7 days.

Alpinia zerumbet
GINGER FLOWER

Buy when flowers look fresh and upright. Re-cut stem ends and place in tepid water. Avoid draughts and display in warm temperatures, out of direct sunlight. Lasts 8 to 10 days.

Anethum graveolens or Peucedanum graveolens
DILL

Buy when flowers are open and place in water immediately. The stems are hollow, and large stems (although not necessarily smaller ones) benefit from being filled with water and plugged. Full flowers last up to 7 days.

Angiozanthos species
KANGAROO PAW (Red: **Angiozanthos rufus**; yellow: **Angiozanthos flavidus**)

Buy when in full flower. Responds well to stem ends being cut frequently (this helps prevent flowers from drying out) and to tepid water treatment. Lasts up to 10 days.

Anthurium andraeanum
ARTIST'S PALETTE, PAINTER'S PALETTE OR FLAMINGO FLOWER (Dark chocolate: **'Choco'**; apple green: **'Midori'**; green, white and reddish pink: **'Paradiso'**)

This tropical plant does not produce true flowers but modified leaves, or spathes, which resemble flowers – these are usually heart shaped and shiny, with a cylindrical spadix or tube in the centre. Responds well to warm conditions. Keep out of draughts and away from direct or excessive heat. Lasts up to 2 weeks.

Arundinaria
BAMBOO

The leaves of this grass are prone to drying and curling, but misting aids longevity. Display in cool temperatures out of direct heat and sunlight. Lasts 5 to 7 days; as a stem, without leaves, lasts for several months or even years.

Asclepias tuberosa
MILKWEED OR ASCLEPIAS

Buy when the majority of the flowers on the cluster are open – dying florets do not fall off, so after about 3 days some may look tired and sad while others have yet to open. You can cut off dead florets with a pair of scissors. Keep away from excessive heat and draughts. Lasts up to 7 days.

Aspidistra elatior
ASPIDISTRA

Tolerant indoor and outdoor plant, which thrives in cool, shady conditions. Can withstand low temperatures and low light levels, as well as heat and dust. Foliage used in cut-flower arrangement will last for several weeks.

Astilbe
ASTILBE

Buy in full flower. Bleeds when cut: use searing or hot water treatment. Leaves tend to die before the flowers – remove them as they wilt and shrivel (this will also extend vase life). Lasts 5 to 7 days.

Bupleurum
BUPLEURUM

Buy when flowers have a strong, fresh green appearance. The soft stems respond to conditioning with tepid water. Keep out of direct heat and sunlight. Lasts up to 7 days.

Chrysanthemum indicum hybrids
CHRYSANTHEMUM (Single-headed green flower: 'Shamrock')

Wide selection available, from the standard single-headed chrysanthemums to the multi-headed or spray chrysanthemums – all come in a wide range of colours and shapes. The firm to woody stems respond well to hot water treatment. Do not add cut-flower food to the water. Keep out of direct heat. Lasts up to 14 days.

Chrysanthemum leucanthemum
OX-EYE DAISY

Buy when flowers are open. Responds to tepid water treatment. Keep away from direct heat. Lasts up to 10 days.

Convallaria majalis
LILY OF THE VALLEY

If on the root, keep wrapped in damp paper until ready to use. As a cut flower, cut off white part of stem and place in shallow, tepid water. Lasts 4 to 5 days.

Cydonia oblonga
QUINCE

Buy when buds are just about to open. Responds to hot water treatment. Full flowers last 5 to 7 days; if forced to flower from bud stage in a warm room, lasts 3 to 4 weeks.

Cymbidium cultivars
CYMBIDIUM

Range of orchids available in a selection of colours. Large plants have between 8 and 12 individual flowers on one spike; miniature flowers are about half the size of the normal flowers – which are approximately 10 cm (4 in). Buy when most of the flowers on the spike are open, with the top bud just starting to open. Usually sold in a vial or plastic tube – remove and re-cut stem. Responds to flower food. Keep away from ethylene gas (emitted by wilting flowers and ripening fruit) and excessive heat. Lasts about 14 days.

Cynara scolymus
CYNARA OR GLOBE ARTICHOKE

This decorative herbaceous plant is also grown as a vegetable. Buy as buds start to open and show a little colour. The hard-to-woody stems respond to hot water treatment. Buds are also attractive in displays. A good plant for drying. Lasts 7 to 10 days.

Cyperus alternifolius
UMBRELLA PLANT OR CROWN PALM

Buy when firm and green with the leaf flat, not curled. Place in water and keep in cool conditions. Lasts 5 to 7 days.

Cyperus papyrus
PAPYRUS

Re-cut stems and place in clean water; do not add cut-flower food. Display in a cool and ventilated but not draughty place. Lasts 5 to 7 days.

Dahlia species and types
DAHLIA

Buy when flowers are half- to three-quarters open. Do not buy if back petals are shrivelled. The stems are hollow, and large stems benefit from being filled with water and plugged. Give smaller stems tepid water treatment. Lasts 3 to 5 days.

Delphinium cultorum cultivars

DELPHINIUM (Blue with white bee: **'Bluebird'**; mauve pink: **'Astolat'**; pale mauve with white bee: **'Guinivere'**; white: **'Galahad'**) The largest spikes are produced from Pacific hybrids. Buy when the flowers on the spike are three-quarters open. The stems are hollow, and large stems benefit from being filled with water and plugged. Display in cool temperatures to extend vase life. Lasts 3 to 7 days.

Dianthus barbatus

SWEET WILLIAM

Buy when flowers are almost fully open. Re-cut stems regularly. Likes tepid water conditioning. Lasts up to 7 days in fresh water.

Dianthus caryophyllus hybrids

CARNATION (Gold: **'Harvest Moon'**; pink: **'Sorento'**; red: **'Scania'**) Keep away from ethylene gas (emitted by wilting flowers and ripening fruit) and excessive heat. Benefits from good air-circulation. Lasts up to 3 weeks, if properly cared for.

Dicentra spectablis

BLEEDING HEART

Re-cut stem ends, place in tepid water and keep out of direct heat. Lasts 5 to 7 days.

Epimedium

BARRENWORT or **BISHOP'S HAT**

Re-cut stem ends. Condition for up to 2 hours in tepid water before use. Keep away from direct heat. Lasts up to 5 days, although young leaves can curl up if kept in very dry or hot conditions.

Eremurus

FOXTAIL LILY

Buy when flower spike is half open. The soft stems are susceptible to bacteria: use a bacteriacide. Re-cut stem ends and change the water frequently. Lasts up to 7 days.

Eryngium alpinum

STEEL THISTLE

Buy when flowers are open and showing colour. Condition the semi-hard stems with tepid water treatment and then add a good cut-flower food. Easy subject to display. Lasts 7 to 10 days.

Eucalyptus globulus

EUCALYPTUS OR **GUM TREE** OR **AUSTRALIAN GUM TREE**

Easy to look after. Re-cut stem ends and use tepid water treatment. Some species have strong Eucalyptus smell. Lasts 10 to 14 days.

Eucharis grandiflora 'Amazonica'

AMAZON LILY

Buy when first flowers are starting to open and show colour – handle with care, as the flowers bruise easily. The firm stems are best conditioned with tepid water treatment. For maximum vase life, keep at a temperature 7°C to 10°C (45°F to 50°F) in high humidity. Lasts 7 to 10 days – some flowers will die while new ones continue to open.

Euphorbia

SPURGE (Lime green flowers: **'Purpurea'**)

Buy when flowers are open and stems look fresh and turgid. Wear gloves as this plant is a latex sap producer. Condition with either hot water treatment or by searing stems with a flame. Lasts 7 to 10 days.

Forsythia x *intermedia*

FORSYTHIA OR **GOLDEN BELL** (Bright yellow: **'Spectabilis'**; golden yellow: **'Lynwood'**)

Buy when flowers are closed, with the smallest amount of colour showing. Condition the woody stems with hot water treatment, then place in tepid water to extend vase life. Display in as cool a temperature as possible. Lasts 5 to 10 days.

Fritillaria meleagris

FRITILLARY

The soft stems are susceptible to bacteria: use a bacteriacide. Re-cut stem ends and change water frequently. Lasts 5 to 7 days.

Galanthus nivalis

SNOWDROP

The soft stems respond to tepid water treatment. Use a cut-flower food for bulbs. Lasts up to 7 days.

Geranium renardii
OUTDOOR GERANIUM
Buy when flowers are starting to open. Re-cut stem ends. A soft-stemmed subject that responds to tepid water treatment. Keep at about 12°C (54°F). Lasts 4 to 5 days.

Gerbera jamesonii hybrids
GERBERA OR TRANSVAAL DAISY OR BARBERTON DAISY
Condition the firm stems with tepid water treatment and use a bacteriacide. Stems block easily, so cut 10mm (approx. 1/2in) off them every other day. If flower heads become limp, wrap them in newspaper and then immerse up to the neck in deep water for at least 5 hours. Lasts up to 7 days.

Gloriosa superba 'Rothschildiana'
GLORY LILY OR FLAME LILY
Buy when the perianth segments (the outer parts of the flower) are arched and the stamens stand away from the stigma. Responds well to plant food. If flowers go limp, submerge in water for about 6 hours or until firm. Lasts for up to 10 days if kept in cool conditions.

Hamamelis mollis
WITCH HAZEL
Buy when flowers are open. Re-cut the woody stems and condition using hot water treatment. Lasts up to 7 days. However, if cut in dormancy, and forced to flower in a warm room, lasts up to 4 weeks.

Helianthus annuus and *Helianthus decapetalus*
SUNFLOWER (Bright yellow: 'Elite Sun')
Buy when the flowers are already open. The flower benefits from tepid water treatment. Lasts up to 10 days if kept in cool temperatures.

Heliconia
LOBSTER CLAW
Can be divided into erect types and hanging types (Erect: *Heliconia elongata*, *Heliconia humilis*; hanging: *Heliconia pendula*).
Keep above 10°C (50°F) as cold conditions can discolour the flowers. Lasts up to 2 weeks.

Hippeastrum cultivars
AMARYLLIS OR BELLADONNA LILY (Peachy pink: 'Appleblossom'; plummy red: 'Hercules'; white: 'Ludwig Dazzler')
The flower usually bought in florists and used in this book is Hippeastrum, which is closely related to, and frequently known as, amaryllis. The hollow stems benefit from being filled with water and plugged. Cut 25mm (1in) off stem ends every 4 days. Lasts up to 10 days as flowers open and a further 7 days when fully open.

Hyacinthoides non-scripta (Scilla)
BLUEBELL OR WILD HYACINTH
Buy when flowers are starting to open. Use tepid water treatment. Lasts 5 to 7 days.

Hydrangea macrophylla
HYDRANGEA (OR HORTENSIA) MOP HEAD
Buy when showing a lot of colour. As a plant, keep compost damp (hydrangeas can wilt quickly). As a cut flower, use tepid water treatment and a plant food. If flower wilts, place stem and head upside-down in cold water; leave for up to 2 hours. Lasts up to 7 days.

Iris cultivars
IRIS
Most bought irises are cultivars of Dutch hybrids (Blue: 'Ideal'; purple: 'Professor Blaauw'; white: 'Casablanca' and 'White Excelsior'; yellow: 'Golden Harvest').
Buy when flower has colour but not fully open. If tip of bud is dry, it will not open properly. Cut off white part of stem. Re-cut stem ends frequently. Keep away from ethylene gas (emitted by wilting flowers and ripening fruit) and excessive heat. Lasts up to 7 days.

Jasminum
JASMINE
Difficult to find as a cut flower but readily available as a pot plant. Water well before cutting. Highly perfumed and delicate flowers. Display in water in a cool place. Lasts 2 to 3 days.

Juncus effusus
CORKSCREW RUSH
Mist to keep in good condition. Display in a cool place in shallow water. Lasts 5 to 7 days.

Lathyrus odoratus cultivars
SWEET PEA

Buy when flowers are closed or just showing colour – buying in full bloom will reduce vase life by up to 2 days. Handle with care because petals will bruise easily when open. Responds to tepid water treatment. Keep away from ethylene gas (emitted by wilting flowers and ripening fruit) and excessive heat. Lasts between 3 and 5 days.

Lavandula species
LAVENDER

Buy when over half the flowers on the spike are open. Condition with tepid water treatment. Lasts up to 10 days.

Leucojum aestivum
SNOWFLAKE FLOWER OR **LONDON LILY**

Buy or cut from the garden as first flower opens. Responds to tepid water treatment. Lasts up to 5 days.

Lilium cultivars
LILY

Buy as first buds start to show colour. Re-cut stem ends and use tepid water treatment. Lasts up to 14 days.

Malus floribunda 'Golden Hornet'
CRAB APPLE

Buy when fruits are just starting to colour; they will slowly turn golden yellow. Use a plant food suitable for hard wood or shrub stems. If leaves start to shrivel, remove and allow the decorative fruits to ripen. Lasts up to a month in cool conditions.

Matthiola incana
HOARY STOCK OR **GILLYFLOWER**

Buy when flower spike is half open. This plant is susceptible to the production of bacteria in the water, so use a bacteriacide and change the water regularly. It will last up to 7 days if properly cared for.

Monstera deliciosa
MONSTER LEAF OR **SWISS CHEESE PLANT** OR **CERIMAN**

Buy when leaves look fresh; do not buy if there are signs of dark brown to black blotches on leaves, or if the tips of the leaves appear dry. Condition using tepid water treatment. Lasts 7 to 14 days.

Muscari armeniacum
GRAPE HYACINTH

Buy when floret at base of flower spike is just showing colour. Condition with tepid water treatment and keep away from heat or direct sunlight. Lasts 5 to 6 days.

Narcissus species and cultivars
NARCISSUS

Buy when in bud (narcissi open quickly when brought into warm temperatures). Best displayed on their own as they exude a sticky sap, which can affect other flowers by blocking the cells in their stems. For best results, change water after 24 hours. Lasts 4 to 6 days.

Nelumbo nucifera
LOTUS SEEDHEAD

The firm stems are best conditioned with tepid water treatment. Keep in warm but not hot conditions. Lasts 5 to 7 days.

Nymphaea capensis
BLUE WATER LILY

Buy as flowers start to show colour. A water plant that does not like hot or dry conditions. Best displayed at about 12°C to 15°C (54° to 60°F) in plenty of water. Mist regularly to reduce effects of transpiration. Lasts 5 to 7 days.

Oncidium
ONCIDIUM ORCHID OR **DANCING LADY ORCHID** (Yellow: 'Bridal Shower')

Buy when flower spray is about three-quarters open with some buds still at the tip. Can also be bought as a plant. Flowers prone to dropping if placed in very cool conditions. Keep out of direct heat and condition with hot water treatment. Lasts up to 7 days.

Ornithogalum arabicum
BLACK-EYED STAR OF BETHLEHEM

Buy when about one-third of florets are open. Keep away from ethylene gas (emitted by wilting flowers and ripening fruit) and direct heat. Lasts up to 14 days.

Paeonia
PEONY

Buy when flowers are showing colour but in bud or half-bud stage. Responds well to tepid water treatment. Lasts up to 8 days if kept in a cool place.

Papaver 'Maxi'
POPPY

Buy when pods are blue-green with an over-bloom (a thin grey layer which forms on plant and indicates it is in good condition). Easy to look after and responds to tepid water treatment. Lasts up to 10 days.

Papaver nudicaule
ICELAND POPPY

Buy when petals are just starting to break from the bud. Cut off a small amount of stem, condition with tepid water treatment and use an appropriate plant food. Lasts up to 5 days.

Paphiopedilum or *Cypripedium*
SLIPPER ORCHID OR LADIES' SLIPPER ORCHID

Buy when flowers are open. Often comes in a vial or tube – remove this covering and re-cut stem. Best kept between 10°C and 12°C (50°F to 54°F). Avoid draughts and excessive heat. Lasts up to 10 days.

Phyllostachys
BAMBOO

Likes cool temperatures and a lot of light. Water when soil dries out. Lasts 5 to 7 days; as a stem, without leaves, lasts for several months or even years.

Physalis alkekengi 'Franchetii'
CHINESE LANTERN OR CAPE GOOSEBERRY

Buy when pods are just beginning to show colour. The semi-woody stems respond well to hot water treatment. Lasts 7 to 10 days. Good for drying if hung upside-down before heads start to droop.

Polianthes tuberosa
TUBEROSA

Buy when first flowers are starting to open. A highly fragrant flower. Responds to tepid water treatment. Lasts up to 14 days.

Populus tremula
ASPEN

Can be displayed in water or as a dried subject. If displayed in water, buds will eventually open. Twigs are tolerant of all conditions.

Prunus
CHERRY BLOSSOM

Buy when buds are just opening. The woody stems respond well to hot water treatment and being placed in tepid water with cut-flower food. Keep out of direct heat. Lasts up to 7 days if bought in flower; however, if bought in cold months and forced to flower in a warm room, lasts up to 8 weeks (it will be in flower for 6 of these 8 weeks), but water must be changed regularly.

Ranunculus acris
BUTTERCUP

Condition the soft stems with tepid water treatment. Keep out of direct heat and sunshine. Lasts about 3 days before petals start to fall (although other buds will open); total vase life of 5 to 6 days.

Rosa cultivars
ROSE

A wide selection of flower types and petal counts in a large range of colours (soft gold bi-colour with red edge: **'Ambience'**; deep red: **'Danse de feu'**; pink/red with silvery white reverse to petal: **'Nicole'**). Buy when in half-open to open bud. If in doubt, buy when open, as some buds may never develop. Susceptible to bacteria: needs clean water and a bacteriacide. Responds well to hot water treatment and cut-flower food added to the water. Keep out of direct heat. If flower heads become limp, wrap them in newspaper and then immerse up to the neck in deep water for at least 5 hours. Lasts about 14 days.

Rudbeckia nitida
CONE FLOWER

Buy when flowers are starting to open. Keep away from direct heat and sunlight. If flower heads become limp, wrap them in newspaper and then immerse up to the neck in deep water for up to 2 hours. Lasts 6 to 7 days.

Salix caprea
PUSSY WILLOW

Useful as a fresh or dried stem. Easy to look after, likes cool conditions and will eventually grow roots in the water.

Salix contorta
CORKSCREW WILLOW OR CONTORTED WILLOW

Useful as a fresh or dried stem. Easy to look after, likes warm conditions and will eventually grow roots in the water. If cut fresh in the cold months of the year lasts up to a month. When dried lasts indefinitely.

Scabiosa caucasica
SCABIOUS

Buy when flowers are starting to open. Re-cut stem ends frequently. Delicate flowers: keep away from direct sunlight, draughts and excessive heat. Lasts 5 to 6 days.

Solidago
GOLDEN ROD

Buy when first few flowers are starting to turn yellow but overall spike is green. Re-cut stem ends and give warm water treatment. Lasts up to 7 days.

Strelitzia reginae
BIRD-OF-PARADISE FLOWER

Buy when first flowers are opening. Re-cut stem ends regularly. As orange flower spike dies, carefully cut a slit down open part of pod, ease out the fresh flowers and fan out. Lasts between 10 and 14 days.

Syringa vulgaris cultivars
LILAC (Lilac/rose: **'Lavaliensis'**; pale lavender: **'Herman Eilers'**; white: **'Madame Florent Stepman'**)

Buy when flower spikes are starting to open. Hot water treatment with plant food added can extend vase life. Likes a lot of water. Lilac sap can shorten the vase life of other flowers – but if mixing with other flowers, do not re-cut stem end and leave to stand on its own for 24 hours before use. Lasts up to 7 days.

Triteleia peduncularis
BRODIAEA

Buy when flowers are just beginning to open. Keep at a temperature of about 12°C (54°F). Lasts 7 to 10 days; as some flowers die, others will open.

Tulipa species and cultivars
TULIP

A huge range of cultivars are available through most of the colour spectrum (bright yellow: **'Yokohama'**; orange with yellow edge: **'Kees Nelis'**; pink with white base: **'Blenda'**; red: **'Prominence'**). Buy when in bud. Likes plenty of water and will continue to grow for the first 2 days in water. Cut-flower food is beneficial to the full opening of the flower. Curves toward the light, so display in an evenly-lit spot. Lasts up to 3 days in the opening stage and a further 4 to 5 days when fully open.

Viburnum fragrans
VIBURNUM

Outdoor shrub with woody stems. Responds well to hot water treatment and special plant food for woody-stemmed cut flowers. Lasts up to 7 days when open. If cut when in tight bud and forced open in warm conditions, lasts 3 weeks in various stages of development.

Viburnum opulus 'Sterile'
GUELDER ROSE OR SNOWBALL BUSH

Buy when flowers are greenish – they will open and eventually turn white, unless restricted by their vase life. Re-cut stem ends and condition with hot water treatment. Responds to plant food for woody-stemmed subjects. Keep out of direct heat. Lasts up to 7 days.

Viburnum tinus
PURPLE-BERRIED VIBURNUM

Re-cut stem ends. Shrubby subject that likes hot water treatment. Keep away from direct heat. Change water regularly. Lasts up to 14 days.

Xanthorrhoea australis
STEEL GRASS
Keep cool and prevent from drying out as this will reduce vase life. Lasts up to 14 days.

Zantedeschia species and cultivars
CALLA LILY OR **ARUM LILY** (dark purple to black: 'Schwarzwalder'; orange to blood red: **'Mango'**; purple to pinkish red: *rehmannii* cultivars; white: *aethiopica*)
Re-cut stem ends and use cut-flower food. Lasts up to 14 days at 8°C to 15°C (46°F to 59°F), fewer at higher temperatures.

POTTED PLANTS

Agave americana
AMERICAN ALOE
In mild climates, will tolerate being outside in warm months, but is not frost-tolerant – best in a conservatory or well-lit room. Keep above 12°C (54°F). Do not over-water, particularly in cold months. Large, sharp spikes along the edges of the thick leaves, so keep away from children and pets.

Agave victoriae-reginae
AGAVE
A desert succulent that likes temperatures above 12°C (54°F). Do not over-water. Keep out of draughts.

Aloe vera
ALOE, MEDICINE PLANT OR **BURN PLANT**
From the succulent family and found in dryish climates. If kept in a pot, use a good standard compost with added sharp grit. Likes warm, bright conditions. Tolerates direct sunlight but not for the whole day. Do not over-water.

Arundaria
BAMBOO *See page 203*

Carex
SEDGE
Most are cool-temperature lovers and best between 8°C and 10°C (46°F to 50°F). Water frequently but do not allow to sit in water.

Cocos nucifera
COCONUT PALM
Easily-cared-for houseplant. Best above 15°C (59°F) with a good amount of natural light. Keep compost damp. Water regularly in warm conditions.

Cupressus macrocarpa 'Goldcrest'
GOLDEN CUPRESSUS
Easily grown. To retain topiary effect, trim about 2 or 3 times a year. Best displayed indoors in cool temperatures (strictly, this is an outdoor plant). Water when compost dries out.

Echinocactus grusonii
GOLDEN BARREL CACTUS OR **MOTHER-IN-LAW'S SEAT**
A good conservatory or house-plant cactus. Withstands some neglect. Tolerates high temperatures: most are best suited to a temperature of above 12°C (54°F). Correct watering is crucial if they are to thrive: reduce to virtually no watering at all when temperatures are low; increase to watering once a week when temperatures rise slightly and through warm months and growing period.

Eichhorina crassipes
BLUEBELL OR **WATER HYACINTH**
Suitable for home or conservatory. Thrives in warm conditions with temperatures no lower than 15°C (59°F). Copes with full sun but is best with a little shade in a well-lit space. Likes humid conditions and misting regularly. A shallow bowl filled with water makes a suitable habitat.

Euphorbia eritraea
EUPHORBIA
A dry climate euphorbia. Best in 12°C (54°F) and above. Reduce watering in cold months; increase when temperatures get warmer. Display in well-lit space, out of direct sunlight.

Ficus benjamina
WEEPING FIG
Easy-to-grow houseplant. Best in a conservatory or well-lit room but out of direct sun. Keep at 12°C (54°F) or above. Water when compost dries out and feed regularly.

Hydrangea macrophylla

HYDRANGEA (OR **HORTENSIA**) **MOP HEAD** *See page 201*

Laurus nobilis

BAY TREE

A wonderful plant that tolerates a few degrees of frost but is best in a cool but frost-free area. Slow-growing but easy to train into shapes and a good subject for topiary work. Feed about once every 14 days with a general liquid feed.

Ligustrum japonicum

SMALL-LEAFED PRIVET

Outdoor subject best displayed indoors in well-lit, cool conditions. Needs regular watering and feeding.

Phalaenopsis

MOTH ORCHID OR **BUTTERFLY ORCHID** (Pink: *schilleriana* **hybrids**; White: *amabilis* **hybrids**)

An epyphite which grows high on branches in tropical rain forests. Gains most of its moisture through its aerial roots. Likes specialist orchid compost nutrient with a very coarse texture, and free and open drainage. Keep between 10°C and 15°C (50°F to 59°F).

Phyllostachys

BAMBOO *See page 203*

Platycerium bifurcatum

STAG'S HORN FERN

Suitable for home or conservatory. Likes compost with a very coarse texture and free and open drainage. Thrives in temperatures above 15°C (59°F). Tolerates full sun but best in partial shade. Moderate watering (once a week) is adequate in temperatures between 15° and 18°C (59° and 64°F). Benefits from misting or humid atmosphere.

INDEX OF FLOWERS AND PLANTS

Page numbers refer to the pages in the main part of the book on which the photograph of the relevant flower is shown.

picture credits

The publishers would like to thank the following people and photographic libraries for permission to reproduce their material. Every care has been taken to trace copyright holders. However, if we have omitted anyone we apologize for this and will, if informed, make corrections in any future edition

Page 1 David Hiscock/DBP **5** David Hiscock/DBP **6** DBP **7** DBP **14–15** David Hiscock/DBP **18** David Hiscock/DBP **19** David Hiscock/DBP **20** David Hiscock/DBP **21** David Hiscock/DBP **22–3** Ed Reeve/The Interior Archive **24** Winfried Heinze/Red Cover **25** David Hiscock/DBP **26** David Hiscock/DBP **27** David Hiscock/DBP **28** Andrew Twort/Red Cover **29** David Hiscock/DBP **30** Andreas von Einseidel/Red Cover **31** Andreas von Einseidel/Red Cover **32 left and right** Winfried Heinze/Red Cover **34** DBP **35** DBP **36** Winfried Heinze/Red Cover **37 top** Andreas von Einseidel/Red Cover **37 bottom** Jacqui Hurst **38** David Hiscock/DBP **39** David Hiscock/DBP **40** Ken Hayden/Red Cover **41 left** Ken Hayden/Red Cover **41 right** Ken Hayden/Red Cover **42–3** Andrew Wood/DBP **46** Andrew Wood/DBP **47** Andrew Wood/DBP **48** Ray Main/Mainstream **49 both** Ray Main/Mainstream **50** David Hiscock/DBP **51** David Hiscock/DBP **52** F.B. Barehardt/Camera Press **53** David Loftus/Tony Stone/Getty **54** R. Stradtwaum/Camera Press **55** Nadia Mackenzie/The Interior Archive **56 top** Ray Main/Mainstream **56 bottom** Nadia Mackenzie/The Interior Archive **57** Verne/Houses and Interiors **58** David Hiscock/DBP **59** David Hiscock/DBP **60** Winfried Heinze/Red Cover **61** Fairlady/Camera Press **62** Nadia Mackenzie/The Interior Archive **63 top and bottom** M. Cogliantry/DBP **64 both** David Hiscock/DBP **65** David Hiscock/DBP **66** Paul Ryan/International Interiors **67 both** Simon Upton/The Interior Archive **68–9** David Hiscock/DBP **72** Ray Main/Mainstream **73** Ray Main/Mainstream **74 both** David Hiscock/DBP **75** David Hiscock/DBP **76–7** David Hiscock/DBP **78** Nicholas Bruant/The Interior Archive **79 both** Nicholas Bruant/The Interior Archive **80** K. Eulenberg/Camera Press **81** Ray Main/Mainstream **82** Winfried Heinze/Red Cover **83** Ed Reeve/The Interior Archive **84** Andrew Wood/DBP **85** Andrew Wood/DBP **86** Winfried Heinze/Red Cover **87** James Mitchell/Red Cover **88 both** Richard Glover/VIEW **89** Richard Glover/VIEW **90 both** Ray Main/Mainstream **91** Ray Main/Mainstream **92** David Hiscock/DBP **93** David Hiscock/DBP **94–5** David Hiscock/DBP **98** Paul Ryan/International Interiors **99** Paul Ryan/International Interiors **100** Christopher Drake/Red Cover **101** Brian Harrison/Red Cover **102 both** Christopher Drake/Red Cover **103** Elizabeth Whiting Associates **104** David Hiscock/DBP **105** David Hiscock/DBP **106** Flowers & Foliage **107 top** Paul Ryan/International Interiors **107 bottom** Alan Weintraub/Arcaid **108 both** Christopher Drake/Red Cover **110** Andrew Twort/Red Cover **111 left** Andrew Wood/The Interior Archive **111 right** Christopher Drake/Red Cover **112** David Hiscock/DBP **113** David Hiscock/DBP **114** Ray Main/Mainstream **115** M. Cogliantry/DBP **116** David Hiscock/DBP **117** David Hiscock/DBP **118** Nadia Mackenzie/The Interior Archive **119** Ray Main/Mainstream **120–1** David Hiscock/DBP **124** David Hiscock/DBP **125** David Hiscock/DBP **126** Ken Hayden/Red Cover **127** Ken Hayden/Red Cover **128** David Hiscock/DBP **129** David Hiscock/DBP **130–1** David Hiscock/DBP **132** Verne/Houses and Interiors **133** Verne/Houses and Interiors **134** Camera Press **135** Ray Main/Mainstream **136** Luke White/The Interior Archive **137 both** Ray Main/Mainstream **138 both** James Morris/Axiom **139** James Morris/Axiom **140** Paul Ryan/International Interiors **141** Ed Reeve/The Interior Archive **142** David Hiscock/DBP **143** Ray Main/Mainstream **144** James Morris/Axiom **145** David Hiscock/DBP **146** David Hiscock/DBP **147** David Hiscock/DBP **148** Andreas von Einseidel/Red Cover **149** Andreas von Einseidel/Red Cover **150** Ed Reeve/The Interior Archive **151 left** Richard Bryant/Arcaid **151 right** Ray Main/Mainstream **152 top** Ray Main/Mainstream **152 bottom** Nicholas Kane/Arcaid **153** Grant Smith/VIEW **154** Jake Fitzjones/Red Cover **155** Ken Hayden/Red Cover **156** Peter Cook/VIEW **157** Paul Ryan/International Interiors **158–9** Andrew Wood/DBP **162** Sarie Visi/Camera Press **163** Sarie Visi/Camera Press **164** David Hiscock/DBP **165** David Hiscock/DBP **166** Flowers & Foliage **167** Andrew Wood/The Interior Archive **168** Andrew Wood/DBP **169** Andrew Wood/DBP **170 top** Paul Ryan/International Interiors **170 bottom** Jacqui Hurst **171** Andrew Wood/DBP **172** Paul Ryan/International Interiors **173** David Hiscock/DBP **174** David Hiscock/DBP **175** David Hiscock/DBP **176** David Hiscock/DBP **177** David Hiscock/DBP **178 both** David Hiscock/DBP **179** David Hiscock/DBP **180** David Hiscock/DBP **181** David Hiscock/DBP **182 both** David Hiscock/DBP **183** David Hiscock/DBP **184** David Hiscock/DBP **185** David Hiscock/DBP **186** David Hiscock/DBP **187** David Hiscock/DBP **188** Ray Main/Mainstream **189 both** Fritz von Schulenberg/The Interior Archive **190–1** David Hiscock/DBP **192-3** DBP **194-5** DBP **196-7** DBP

For information on the work and designs of Ou Baholyodhin, readers may visit his website at the following location: www.ou-b.com

Commissioned photography, DBP © 2001, styled by Robert Hornsby of IN WATER: pages 5, 14–15, 18–19, 20–1, 25, 29, 34–5, 50–1, 64–5, 68–9, 74–5, 92–3, 94–5, 104–5, 112–13, 116–17, 124–5, 128–9, 130–1, 145, 146–7, 164–5, 174–5, 176–7, 178–9, 180–1, 182–3, 184–5 and 186–7

IN WATER is a flower design business with a difference. In 1999, Claire Garabedian and Robert Hornsby came together from the worlds of fashion and design with the aim of taking floral display to a new level. In the process they created one of their sleek and inspirational designs of flowers completely submerged in water. You can find out more about IN WATER on their website: **www.inwater.uk.com**

Publisher's acknowledgments

The authors and the publishers would like to thank the following people for their invaluable and kind assistance in the creation of this book: In Water, Tarsem, Vessel, Visionary Living, and Nurit and Isaac Yardeni.

In addition, the publishers would like to extend their special thanks to Hanne Bewernick, Jane Donovan, William Greenwood (National Art Library at the V&A, London), James Hodgson, Diana Loxley and Allan Sommerville

FLOWER IDENTIFICATION: PRELIMINARY PAGES AND CHAPTER OPENERS
Page 1 *Rosa* cultivar **5** *Galanthus Nivalis* **14–15** *Dianthus caryophyllus* hybrids **42–3** *Zantedeschia* 'Schwarzwalder', *Aspidistra elatior* **68–9** *Convallaria majalis* **94–5** *Astilbe* **120–1** *Hyacinthus orientalis* **158–9** *Gloriosa superba* 'Rothschildiana', *Nelumbo nucifera* **190–1** *Tuberosa* **Jacket** *Dahlia* [front], *Zantedeschia* cultivar [back]